BRAND
LIKE A
ROCK STAR

**LESSONS FROM ROCK 'N' ROLL TO
MAKE YOUR BUSINESS RICH AND FAMOUS**

STEVE JONES

GREENLEAF
BOOK GROUP PRESS

Published by Greenleaf Book Group Press
Austin, Texas
www.gbgpress.com

Distributed by Greenleaf Book Group LLC

For ordering information or special discounts for bulk purchases, please contact Greenleaf Book Group LLC at PO Box 91869, Austin, TX 78709, 512.891.6100.

Design and composition by Greenleaf Book Group LLC
Cover design by Greenleaf Book Group LLC
Photos courtesy of Photofest, Inc.

Publisher's Cataloging-In-Publication Data
(Prepared by The Donohue Group, Inc.)
Jones, Steve (Stephen Andrew), 1970-
    Brand like a rock star : lessons from rock 'n' roll to make your business rich and famous/ Steve Jones. — 1st ed.
    p. ; cm.
    ISBN: 978-1-60832-195-7
    1. Branding (Marketing) 2. Success in business. 3. Rock musicians—Marketing. 4. Music trade—Marketing. I. Title.
HF5415.1255 .J66 2011
658.8/27   2011927595

Part of the Tree Neutral® program, which offsets the number of trees consumed in the production and printing of this book by taking proactive steps, such as planting trees in direct proportion to the number of trees used: www.treeneutral.com

TreeNeutral

Printed in the United States of America on acid-free paper

11 12 13 14 15 16 10 9 8 7 6 5 4 3 2 1

First Edition

Tanya,
Rock on!

This book is dedicated to the rock stars in my life:
Sue, Isaac, and Matthew. John Lennon said, "A
dream you dream alone is only a dream. A dream
you dream together is reality." Thank you for making
my reality better than any dream I could have ever
dreamed alone.

CONTENTS

THE OPENING ACT

Brand Like a Rock Star was born on a beautiful night, just southwest of Austin, Texas. The day had been hot, but in March it cools quickly in south Texas once the sun hides behind the hills. Under an umbrella of stars, I relaxed on the patio with a cold beer. A Jimmy Buffett song played quietly from a stereo inside. It amazed me to think of how rich and famous Buffett became thanks to that one simple, little hit song, "Margaritaville." Some musicians create chart-topping hit after hit and never have anywhere near the staying power of Jimmy Buffett.

Meanwhile, Buffett has quietly turned that one song into a massive, million-dollar brand. The Buffett brand includes a chain of restaurants in North America and the Caribbean, an extensive clothing line, endless merchandise, a popular beer, a line of tequila, blenders, footwear, two minor league baseball teams, and of course, a record company. His estimated annual income is more than $100 million a year. Yet Buffett's track record on the charts isn't very impressive:

"Come Monday" struggled to reach number thirty in 1974. Hardly a hit song.

And then "Margaritaville" peaked at number eight in 1977.

Although he recorded many albums between 1977 and 2003, not one Buffett song cracked the top thirty after "Margaritaville" until Alan Jackson's song "It's Five O'clock Somewhere" went to number one on the country charts and topped out at number seventeen on the pop charts. It wasn't a Buffett song per se, but it featured a prominent Buffett appearance as he sang a reply to Jackson's question: "What would Jimmy Buffett do?" That cameo put his name near the top of the charts for the first time in twenty-six years.

Jimmy Buffett isn't just a musician. He's a brand. He is a lifestyle. As I began to ponder the magic behind his career, it became clear that it wasn't just magic at play. Yes, there was karma and circumstance and good fortune, but Buffett made smart decisions that evolved his brand into what it is today. Buffett's experience got me thinking about all the cool branding lessons hidden in the music industry:

▶ The Grateful Dead became one of the highest-grossing bands of their era without ever hitting the charts.

▶ KISS turned merchandising into an art form and demonstrated to the world that being different was far more important than being better.

- ▶ U2 showed how having a message, and living up to it, can create a deep connection with fans.

- ▶ AC/DC built a consistent brand that any business could learn from.

The list goes on and on.

That night on the patio, sipping my beer, before my mind declared the idea crazy, I reserved www.brand-likearockstar.com and created a blog that became, over the course of two years, a popular destination for fans of bands and brands alike. The blog remains my outlet for observations about branding viewed through the lens of the music industry.

The connection between music and business has been the basis for my entire career. Despite failing miserably at every musical instrument I've ever tried to play, I have been fortunate enough to make a living in the music industry. Instead of creating music, I've spent the past twenty-seven years programming music on radio stations in the United States, Canada, and the Caribbean. Getting paid to listen to music is no doubt a dream come true, but the stakes are high. Successful radio stations can make millions while unsuccessful stations can easily go broke. As my career evolved from on-air DJ into management, I was exposed firsthand to the impact a powerful brand can have on success. There is a reason that one radio station wins and another loses while both play essentially the same music. The reason is branding. Powerful brands win. Weak brands lose.

No matter the size or nature of your business, the situation is the same: strong brands make more money, are more likely to survive recessions, and last longer. Weak brands usually fade away quickly. From time to time, some weak brands become successful despite their faults, but usually it is because they are the first in a new product category. Those brands are usually the first to fall when a well-branded competitor attacks. Building a brand has never been easy, and it isn't getting any easier. New products and services are everywhere, and the rise of outsourcing, crowdsourcing, and instant digital communication has removed many traditional barriers that kept new competition from starting out. As the caretakers of brands, those of us who manage and grow businesses are in a tough fight. Throughout my career, whenever things got tough, I listened to music. So let's turn up the tunes and learn what we can from them.

Exploring brands through music is what makes *Brand Like a Rock Star* fun. There are plenty of excellent books on branding, marketing, and advertising. What makes *Brand Like a Rock Star* unique—and hopefully engaging—is that it illustrates the ingredients and best practices of successful brands through fun stories from bands and singers we know and love. I've tried to remain neutral on the bands and artists I've written about. It really doesn't matter whether or not I like their music; all that matters is what they can teach us about building killer brands. Certain artists, such as Buffett, KISS, and the Grateful Dead, turn up more often than others because of the wealth of lessons their experiences can teach us. I've found lessons in all types of music, from classic rock to hip-hop to country. Some of the lessons are vital to a brand's success, and others remind us how we can top the charts in our own businesses.

Brand Like a Rock Star doesn't end with the publication of this book. Every day new songs and bands emerge and share new lessons about what to do, and what not to do, when establishing a brand. Your comments, opinions, and feedback will continue to inspire us all in the never-ending process of building better brands.

▼

DEFINING A BRAND

My wife and I were in London for the first time and eager to fight off the jet lag with some authentic English fish and chips. We didn't want a tourist trap. We were seeking the real thing: a pub where native Londoners went. I turned to my iPhone and opened an app that instantly revealed a list of dozens of restaurants that fit our specifications. A few taps later, and we were looking at a menu, reading customer reviews, and using the built-in GPS to get specific instructions on how to get there from where we stood.

In this digital age, many decisions are made exactly like this. And those decisions have led many people to question the value of investing in a strong brand. Why bother when you can attract customers digitally and directly connect their needs with your service? We now live in a world of digital communities, networks of people who share common interests and passions. Technology has made it easy for people who have a niche interest to communicate with others who share that same interest. Online communities exist for virtually every interest, hobby, product, fad, team, book, and band. Through social media, we are all suddenly connected to one another.

Our daily word-of-mouth observations are very powerful when we choose to hit "send" and share them with our communities. With all of this happening at lightning speed around us, we are being told to invest in Search Engine Optimization (SEO) and social media strategies. There is no shortage of SEO and social media gurus who will tell you that as long as you turn up near the top of a Google search and people are talking about you online, you don't need to worry about building a brand in the traditional sense. They are wrong.

The reality is that having a strong brand has never been more critical. While this digital connectedness has changed the way we communicate, it's also made having a recognizable brand more important than ever before.

Yoga-inspired fashion company Lululemon Athletica fosters communities of yoga enthusiasts and those inspired to live a more active and healthy lifestyle. Whole Foods creates communities of people who want to explore organic and sustainable farming. The new era of connectedness has given brands the opportunity to develop relationships with their customers, and potential customers, in ways never before thought possible. Strong brands form the heart of many of these communities.

The digital age has also created a freeway where there once existed only a one-way street; the transaction of two decades ago was a one-way street between the customer and the business, and if you didn't like what you bought, there was little you could do to express your discontent. You could tell your friends that you didn't like something, but there was little hope that your opinion could have any impact on the business. Today the consumer has the power, making the need for strong brands with positive equity and trust even more pronounced.

We are also faced with more options than ever before — all of them conveniently displayed on our computers or smartphones. Restaurants and stores you didn't know about are brought to life digitally and presented for your consideration. Products you never knew existed are reviewed and recommended by your friends on Facebook. A movie you never thought about seeing becomes the buzz on Twitter and inspires you to head to the theater. All of these immediate choices make strong brands crucial. Now what your brand stands for can make all the difference. Your brand's reputation is what inspires someone to choose you over the dozens of other options he discovered in a Google search. Forget SEO. If a brand that is trusted and powerful appears in a search, it is far more likely to get clicked on than an unknown brand that just happened to optimize the search engine process.

Just because your smartphone app or Google search

gives you twenty nearby Chinese food restaurants, not all of them are brands. Most of them, to the average person, are anonymous names and places. But if one of them has built a strong brand, the choice of where to eat becomes easier. Why take a chance on something you don't know when you know exactly what you'll get at P.F. Chang's China Bistro? It is the known and trusted brands that get clicked on, searched, and patronized.

Starbucks has created a brand strong enough to redefine what a cup of coffee should cost. The line at Starbucks is filled with people ready to spend $5 for a coffee. Across the street at Dunkin' Donuts, a strong brand itself, you can buy a coffee for $1. Is it the coffee that accounts for the price difference or are you paying for the brand?

The Apple brand has turned the release of a new product into a cultural and media event. The 2011 launch of Apple's iPad 2 created more fervor than a major movie studio releasing a new blockbuster with A-list Hollywood stars. The product went on to create what Deutsche Bank called an "insurmountable lead" for Apple in the tablet computer market.

Those who diminish the value of a strong brand are usually mistaken in defining what a brand actually is. They believe brands are logos or locations. They think brands are slogans or positioning statements. They believe brands are their products and services, created and defined by advertising and marketing. And once again, they are wrong.

Brands are not the products and services themselves. While the Apple brand may be very strong, it isn't one particular piece of electronics. The Apple brand is a feeling that goes along with using cutting-edge technology that communicates to the world that you are a certain type of person. Are you a Microsoft fan or an Apple fan? There is a big difference, as any Apple person will tell you. Likewise, The Beatles are not "Hey Jude" or "She Loves You," but rather the culmination of factors that create a perception about the band and their fans. Do you think The Beatles or The Rolling Stones was the greatest rock 'n' roll band of all time? Any hardcore fan of either band will argue their side of that debate.

Brands are not commercials or slogans or positioning statements. As much as companies try to influence how we feel about products through advertising and marketing, the real essence of a brand is decided by the customers and communities. When customers perceive a brand to stand for something, those perceptions are nearly impossible to change. How much money would it take to convince customers to ask for a "tissue" instead of a "Kleenex"? No amount of money could accomplish such a feat.

Brands are so much bigger than businesses, logos, names, and locations. Brands go deeper, beneath the visible surface, and exist in the mind. Brands are essentially perceptions and emotions. They are the feelings and associations that come from interacting with a product or service. People identify themselves through the brands they support. The Cadillac driver sees himself in the brand, just as the Jeep driver sees her reflection in her Wrangler and the Prius driver sees his image in his hybrid.

Only brands that understand and embrace how they are perceived have a shot at becoming legendary. Legendary brands can survive recessions, technological shifts, competition, and generation gaps. These "Rock Star" brands can turn small niches into massive profits. Sometimes, legendary brands can even be brought back from the dead. Legendary brands don't have to be international or even national success stories. While most of the examples that are discussed are widely known companies, some legendary brands are local or regional successes.

Regina Pizzeria in Boston doesn't need outlets across America to be a legendary brand. They are legendary in New England. No matter what the weather is like, there is almost always a line snaking toward the red neon sign at 11½ Thacher Street. Everyone's waiting for the chance to step inside the simple brick building where they've baked pizza in a brick oven since 1926. No doubt their original North End, Boston location is the perfect, stereotypical pizzeria. Trying to recreate that aura in Des Moines, Venice, or Calgary would be ludicrous, and would probably result in just another everyday pizza place instead of the unique experience that is Regina.

In-N-Out Burger has made a point of not expanding beyond locations within a one-day's drive of their head office in south Los Angeles. The very fact that they aren't in every city has made their brand infinitely more powerful. When California-born baseball player Jason Giambi played for the New York Yankees, he would bring teammates to In-N-Out Burger when they embarked on West

Coast road trips! The brand's unique approach has also scored them points with local business leaders normally opposed to fast-food outlets, including those responsible for Fisherman's Wharf in San Francisco, where they were the only fast-food restaurant permitted to develop in the historic area.

Legendary brands don't even need to be regional to be legendary. There are countless mom-and-pop stores, small restaurants, and personal services in every town and city that have established themselves as legendary brands within their market. These are the little guys who have taken on the Walmarts and Home Depots of the world and won, in large part because they established themselves as a legendary *local* brand. No matter how large or how small your business is, you have the opportunity to turn it into a legendary brand. It isn't easy, but building greatness never is. Along the way you might have to walk away from what appears to be easy money. You will suffer short-term pain for the proverbial long-term gain. You might have to change your plans dramatically as you go, and you'll probably end up somewhere far away from where the first draft of your business plan said you'd be. That's okay.

Using stories from some of rock 'n' roll's greatest bands, *Brand Like a Rock Star* can give you valuable insight into exactly how to build your brand into a legend. Rock on.

CHAPTER ONE

AC/DC AND THE ART
OF CONSISTENCY

G reatness begins with a clear identity and consistency. One band that truly understood their identity from the very beginning was AC/DC. For more than thirty years, AC/DC has been doing their thing, never wavering from their mission despite trends and fads. Love them or hate them, it doesn't matter: Everyone knows what AC/DC is all about. AC/DC sings about rock 'n' roll, partying, womanizing, driving fast, and having fun. And little else. That identity spans generations, with plenty of songs about shakin', drinkin', movin', screamin', partyin', and of course, rockin'.

They've never recorded a song about social injustice in the developing world. You won't find a single song in the catalog about the angst that burns deep inside the heart of a man as he tries to tell the woman he loves how he really feels. And they have so far resisted the urge to use Auto-Tune or a drum machine or even a keyboard for that matter. On the sixteen albums AC/DC released between 1974 and 2010, there are twenty songs that include the word "rock" in the title. Count 'em.

Only Air Supply, another band from Down Under, has been able to state their brand so clearly in the titles of their songs. Remember Air Supply? Air Supply is AC/DC's musical antithesis, but they were equally consistent in their day. They serenaded the world, and strategically worked the word "love" into nearly every song they came up with. In the early '80s, there's a good chance you slow danced to some of their classics, such as "All Out of Love," "Lost in Love," "Making Love Out of Nothing at All," "The One That You Love," "Young Love," and "The Power of Love."

AC/DC is a stellar example of a band that knows what their fans expect, and they deliver it time after time. Yet while their music is simple, not for a moment should it be inferred that AC/DC isn't creative or unique. They have taken chances and recorded some unusual songs that haven't *exactly* fit the mold. But the biggest risk AC/DC took was having the courage to continue to create their unique sound time and time again, album after album, even when trends and fashions were working against them. Consistent—that's what AC/DC has been for more than thirty years, and it hasn't always been easy.

It takes immense skill and focus to be that consistent, creating an endless supply of driving and powerful straight-ahead rock 'n' roll songs that grab your attention and squeeze tight. Brian Johnson, the lead screamer in AC/DC, once astutely commented that although guitarist Angus Young gets some criticism for creating simple guitar riffs, he should actually be revered for his simplicity. Writing simple, memorable, and powerful music is a rare skill. To paraphrase Johnson, plenty of people hear songs like "Taxman" by The Beatles and think, "That's simple. I could have written that. Sure, but they didn't."

Keeping things brilliantly simple wasn't an accident. In 1975, Phil Carson was charged with the task of finding exciting new bands to sign to Atlantic Records, when he saw some raw super-8 video footage of AC/DC playing "Long Way to the Top." He immediately got on the phone and signed this unknown Australian band to a fifteen-album record deal. At that point, Carson said, keeping things straightforward was already the band's mantra. That simplicity was one of the things that attracted Carson to the band—their pure, unadorned, passionate rock 'n' roll.

"The heart of AC/DC is the rhythm," Carson said. "Drummer Phil Rudd is the epitome of what AC/DC is all about. He hits it hard, every time, right on time. He sticks with it. Cliff Williams is a fantastic bass player. And Malcolm Young's rhythm guitar is amazing."

Beyond the riffs and song titles, even AC/DC's look is consistent. Every album since their debut has included the band's name in the same classic font. You can't look at that font without hearing their music. Since replacing Bon Scott in 1980, Brian Johnson has been wearing the same "newsboy" hat, dark jeans, and sleeveless shirt. Angus Young's school boy uniform, complete with white shirt, tie, and shorts, has been a part of his signature look since the band began.

Angus Young's school boy outfit has been part of AC/DC's signature look since the early 1970s.

They never wore glitter, no matter how big David Bowie and the glam rockers got. They never worked a disco beat into their songs like KISS, Rod Stewart, and The Rolling Stones did. In the 1980s, when rock 'n' roll men wore big hair and make up, AC/DC looked exactly as they always have: with straight long hair, without any hair spray. When the 1990s rolled around, and the rock 'n' roll look-du-jour was sloppy and grunge, AC/DC still looked the same. It is almost as if the band exists in its own world, far removed from the factors at play in music and fashion.

AC/DC simply recognizes and respects what their audience expects from them. No wonder they are so successful, even as times change. Their 2008 album *Black Ice*, released thirty-five years after the band formed, went to number one in nineteen countries. That certainly speaks volumes for their place in contemporary music. It wasn't through dumb luck. The band, according to Carson, was always aware of their image and their audience, and they have worked hard to never violate those expectations, even when times were tough.

"When we first brought AC/DC to America, there was a stunning burst of indifference," Carson said. "Atlantic Records was a very forward-looking company, and they thought we were nuts to sign them because the band was so straight-ahead rock 'n' roll." Yet AC/DC persevered through the initial resistance, winning over audiences, and their record company, one passionate straight-ahead rock 'n' roll song after another.

The initial push-back was strong. Progressive rock was the flavor of the time. The record company wasn't eager to push a raw rock band to radio stations and promoters were reluctant to book them. But as the band persistently played live night after night, eventually Phil Carson started getting positive reviews about his Australian discovery, including one on the Philadelphia radio station WMMR that claimed "AC/DC doesn't just rock 'n' roll, they *are* rock 'n' roll."

In the minds of their fans, AC/DC owns a piece of their mental real estate, which is as valuable as a Manhattan condo or ocean frontage in Santa Monica. We all have a limited amount of brain space reserved for things we care about. We only remember a few brands of shoes, breakfast cereals, dishwashing soaps, furniture stores, and other products. We can't possibly remember all of the brands that compete for our attention, so the brands that occupy our mental real estate are fortunate. AC/DC is one of the music industry's greatest examples of a band that has claimed their mental real estate and refuses to let go.

In the mid-1980s, when hard rock bands had long hair and wore make-up, AC/DC suddenly seemed out of touch. Sales for their albums *Flick of the Switch* and *Fly on the Wall* were disappointing, and many thought the band was finished. Carson remembered seeing the band during those trying times, playing a concert at Nassau Coliseum on Long Island with only eight thousand people in the audience. There were as many empty seats as filled ones. Yet AC/DC played like it was a packed house because they knew they had to meet the expectations of those eight thousand people. To AC/DC, there was no "phoning it in." It isn't just their sound and their look that AC/DC has kept consistent during the past three decades. It's also a commitment to keep the band within the grasp of their fans.

"The band is very conscious of ticket prices and merchandise," Carson said. "They've always tried to keep their concerts accessible to the average fan."

It has paid off. Just like Volvo stands for "safety" and Coldstone Creamery stands for "rich ice cream," AC/DC stands for "straight-ahead rock 'n' roll band." Their iconic logo, stage show, wardrobe, song choices, and every other aspect of their image support their brand. It would be foolish for AC/DC to attempt to change it. Anything other than "straight-ahead rock 'n' roll" from AC/DC just doesn't make sense to their fans.

What would happen if AC/DC changed their look and sound and recorded an Air Supply–like love song? Two things: First, very few of their fans would accept it because it goes against what they know and love. Second, the band would most likely not win over new fans because most non-fans already have a clear idea of what AC/DC is and they don't like it. In fact, when any brand creates a product that isn't congruent with what their fans expect, it interferes with the mental real estate the brand already owns! It diminishes the brand's value.

Unfortunately, that simple truth is lost on many businesses and musicians. The temptation for profit is too great for most brands to resist, and they inevitably compromise the expectations of their customers in an effort to make more money. Business history is littered with stories of brands that pushed their image beyond customer's expectations.

McDonald's deserves a world of credit for building an incredibly strong worldwide brand, and it's done so through amazing consistency. The Big Mac you can buy in Moscow, Idaho, is nearly identical in look, taste, and smell to the Big Mac you can buy in Moscow, Russia. A McDonald's restaurant looks the same no matter where in the world it sits. Behind the counters, the kitchens and equipment are standardized to create a consistent product at a consistent price. Since defining the fast food genre in the 1950s, McDonald's has built an empire driven by consistency. Yet not everything McDonald's has done has been consistent, and it has made some high-profile mistakes. In the early 1990s, McDonald's went on an expensive, ill-fated adventure into pasta and pizza. It renovated restaurants and installed expensive new pizza ovens. Drive-through windows were widened to accommodate pizza boxes. The staff was trained on how to make pizzas, since flipping a burger is different from tossing a pizza.

And then there was the marketing. McDonald's needed to tell the world about its new products, so Mickey D's saturated the North American market with advertising to support the launch of McPizza. Concurrent to the launch of McPizza, the company launched a line of pasta dishes in test markets around America. To go with the McPizza, it peppered the menu with McSpaghetti, lasagna, fettuccine alfredo, and roast chicken. Fortunately, those products didn't make it past the test markets, and they were never rolled out nationwide. The McPizza story is another matter.

Despite the tremendous investment it took and the massive marketing behind it, McPizza never connected with customers. The consensus was that it didn't taste very good, and certainly didn't taste good enough to get people to switch from their preferred pizza place. People interested in pizza and pasta had options, many of them equally as fast as McDonald's and perceived to be of higher quality. Dominoes, Pizza Hut, and others, were top-of-mind with consumers because of their consistency. There was simply no compelling reason for people to think about buying Italian food at McDonald's. Within a few years, McPizza and McPasta dishes disappeared from the menu and the staff went back to doing what they did best: flipping burgers and deep-frying French fries.

Yet a brand must evolve. If a brand remains stagnant in changing times, it runs the risk of becoming irrelevant and out-of-touch with contemporary consumers. The line between growing with consistency and losing brand consistency is a thin one, and one defined by a keen understanding of what the brand represents in the mind of the consumer. It doesn't really matter what the company *thinks* it represents. The only thing that matters is what the brand represents in the consumer's mind: the mental real estate it occupies.

Coors miscalculated its mental real estate in 1990 when it launched Coors Rocky Mountain Spring Water. At the time, Coors wrongly assumed that its brand represented spring water from the Rocky Mountains in the beer-drinking consumer's mind. After all, for more than fifty years it had invested millions of dollars in marketing Coors beer as better than others because it was "brewed with pure Rocky Mountain spring water." That was their slogan. It's what distinguished Coors from the competition:

- ▶ The king of beers (Budweiser)
- ▶ Head for the mountains (Busch)
- ▶ The beer that made Milwaukee famous (Schlitz)
- ▶ It doesn't get any better than this! (Old Milwaukee)
- ▶ It's Miller time! (Miller)

Where Coors went wrong was assuming that because the water made the brand different, it was the essence of the brand, and that essence could be easily transferred to another product. People didn't buy Coors because of the water; they bought Coors because of the great beer that happened to be made with spring water. Coors was, and is, a bottle of beer, not a bottle of water. As a result, Coors Rocky Mountain Spring Water was an expensive flop.

Like AC/DC and sappy love songs, or McDonald's and Italian food, Coors and water didn't mix. If a brand isn't consistent with the expectations of its customers, it fails. There's really no way around it.

What would have happened if Coors had decided to launch Rocky Mountain Spring Water under a different brand name? Pepsi would be happy to tell you. Around the same time that Coors suffered losses from its failed foray into bottled water, Pepsi launched its own bottled water. However, Pepsi's bottled water didn't have the Pepsi brand attached to it. Pepsi's product was called Aquafina, and it launched in 1994 in Kansas and quickly spread across the United States and Canada. Over the next decade, Aquafina became the top-selling bottled water brand in the United States and a leading brand worldwide. Coca-Cola took notice, and in 1999 launched Dasani—its own extremely successful brand of bottled water.

Had Coors better understood its slice of mental real estate the way Pepsi and Coca-Cola did, the world might be a different place for those who drink bottled water. Today Coors could very well have a monopoly on the lucrative bottled water market. Like Pepsi and Coke, Coors already had the production and distribution networks required to launch such a product. What Coors lacked was an understanding of what its brand represented to consumers and potential consumers.

A Rock Star Five-Step Program: Learning AC/DC-Style Consistency

It's easy to look at AC/DC's consistent branding and see how simple it is. So if being consistent is simple, why do so many brands find it difficult? Here are five lessons you can learn from watching AC/DC do it right for over thirty years:

1. **Do what you do.** For AC/DC that was straight-ahead rock 'n' roll: loud, simple power chords, steady backbeats, screaming vocals, and thick guitars.

2. **Study your customers and understand what they think you do.** AC/DC did it night after night, playing live in front of their fans. When you get immediate and direct feedback from 18,000 fans each night, you understand what they want from you.

3. **Live up to your customers' expectations, not your own definition of what you do.** Brian Johnson, AC/DC's lead singer, actually loves musical theatre. In 2003 he started working on a musical version of *Helen of Troy*, in the same style as *Les Miserables*. It was performed in New York in 2005. AC/DC's name never appeared anywhere near it because while Johnson and AC/DC may love Rodgers and Hammerstein and classic musicals, it isn't consistent with their brand.

4. **Commit to your visual cues.** By using the same iconic font and having Angus wear the same schoolboy uniform for decades, the band has created a strong visual-audio association. When you see the AC/DC name in print or see a picture of Angus in that outfit, you can actually hear the band. That's powerful.

continued on following page

5. **Constantly remind your fans what you're about.** With every song, AC/DC drives that message home. It is no coincidence that, after a few years away from the spotlight, they released "Rock and Roll Train" in 2008. Why not use the title of the song to once again remind fans what they're all about?

CHAPTER TWO

▼

CHANGES

The song "Changes" by David Bowie was his personal account of the different directions he was being pulled in. His musical styles were changing; his sexuality was in question; and his Ziggy Stardust personality was emerging. Bowie was aware of the career risks that lay within these changes. He had only recently established himself as a bona fide solo artist with the song "Space Oddity," and he was about to reveal himself under an entirely new identity. He wasn't the first artist to go through these types of changes. One of the rock era's greatest bands went through some major changes themselves, and their experience is a blueprint for brands that face the challenge of evolving without destroying the brand's image.

As discussed in chapter one, great brands are singular

in their focus, always living up to the expectations of their fans. But if that is universally true, how can a company ever expand? What happens when your company comes up with a great new product that you know the world is just waiting for? Do you pass up millions of dollars in revenue to keep a brand's promise?

Of course not! If you are into walking away from millions of dollars in profits, you shouldn't be in business. But simply slapping your existing brand's name on a product that doesn't live up to your customers' expectations is a recipe for failure. Like Coors Rocky Mountain Spring Water and McDonald's pizza, brands cannot expect to succeed if they expand beyond what they represent to their customers and potential customers. That's the lesson learned by one of the biggest rock 'n' roll bands of all time: Passengers.

If they are one of the biggest rock 'n' roll bands of all time, why do you find yourself wondering who this band is? Trust me, you've heard of them, but with a different name. Their story goes back to the late 1970s, when a bunch of high school kids in Ireland got together and jammed. They weren't very good in the beginning, but they kept on practicing and playing. Eventually, they started to refine their sound. They wrote compelling lyrics, sang passionate songs, worked tirelessly on tour, and eventually became very, very famous.

You know the band better as U2.

U2 made their American debut in October 1980. During the next ten years, they sold more than thirty-four million albums, including more than twelve million copies of the 1987 album that many rank as one of rock's greatest albums, *The Joshua Tree.* The band created anthems like "I Still Haven't Found What I'm Looking For," "With or Without You," and "Mysterious Ways."

After the very successful *Achtung Baby* album in 1991, U2 started experimenting with electronic and industrial sounds. They still recorded a fair number of "traditional" U2 hits that their fans responded to. But on *Zooropa,* the band stretched their creative wings beyond what people traditionally thought of as "U2 music." They experimented with industrial and alternative sounds and pushed the technological limits of the studios of the day. As a result of this creative departure, while the album received generally favorable reviews, it didn't sell nearly as well as *Achtung Baby* did, and none of the three singles were substantial hits. The band had created a product (new and unusual electronic music) that wasn't congruent with what their customers expected (the typical and very popular U2 music). While the fans were hoping for Bono's inspiring, soaring vocals and Edge's trademark jangling, ethereal guitar, the band was inspired to go in a much different direction.

The band faced two choices as their post-*Zooropa* creative streak continued. One was to follow their creative muses, and give the world a new U2 album filled with unusual songs. A new U2 album guaranteed a few million copies would be sold to fans who loved the band. This path would allow the band to satisfy their creative desire to experiment with tape loops, rhythm sequencing, computer sounds, sampling, and electronica. They would probably risk continuing to alienate some fans who were already getting turned off by their increasingly experimental music, but they might win over new fans who were intrigued by their new sound.

The other option was to stifle their creativity and record songs their fans expected to hear. It might leave the band creatively unfulfilled, but it would definitely be more profitable. However, U2 are artists. Artists must create. If they had suppressed that need, it probably would have created tension among their members and might've even broken the band up so that each member could pursue his artistic desires. Besides, could the band truly be powerful and relevant if they were creating music for no other reason than making money and satisfying their fans?

The band wisely found a third not-so-obvious option. Instead of alienating their fans with strange music or stifling their own creativity for crass commercialism, they made a very smart decision. They recorded the songs they wanted to, but they never put the U2 name on it. In 1995 they released an album called *Original Soundtracks 1* under the pseudonym Passengers. They didn't promote the album as a U2 project. It was simply a creative outlet project by a group of musicians, not a U2 album. By and large the album was ignored. It was far too eclectic for mainstream tastes. Without the U2 brand name on the cover, it went pretty much unnoticed in music stores. A new eclectic album by a band nobody had ever heard of didn't stand a chance of success. *Original Soundtracks 1* didn't spawn any hits on the radio and Passengers never went on tour. In short, the Passengers project faded and U2 went back to work on a new album called *Pop*.

The brilliance of this strategy was that the band wasn't stigmatized because they had an album flop. Nothing is worse for a high-profile band than a poor-selling album. They didn't suffer any backlash from their fans by releasing a U2 album that sounded nothing like what their fans expected. U2 knew that their fans had certain expectations and that this odd collection of songs wouldn't meet those expectations. So they created a new band, and a whole new brand, with Passengers. It didn't matter that Passengers wasn't particularly successful. The boys didn't need the money, and they got to experiment with new sounds. What mattered was that the project didn't taint the U2 brand.

In hindsight, drummer Larry Mullen acknowledged that *Original Soundtracks 1* crossed the line between interesting music and self-indulgence. Had U2 themselves crossed that line, the effects might have been devastating. They could have seriously eroded their fan base and bruised their image. Instead, no damage was done and U2 as we know it carried on. Shortly after the experimental years of the mid-'90s, U2 publicly acknowledged their experiments and announced that they were "reapplying for the job of the best band in the world." Since then they have gone on to record some of the most compelling music of their career.

In a way, U2 has a lot in common with Honda, Toyota, and Nissan. These three Japanese automakers were faced with a problem in the 1980s. The Japanese government issued Voluntary Export Restraints (VERs) on the auto industry to appease the US government, which was concerned about the Japanese flooding the market with cheaper and more fuel-efficient cars. These export restrictions prevented them from sending more Honda, Toyota, and Nissan cars to America. So the Japanese carmakers sought new opportunities outside of their traditional small car designs. That led all three companies to develop luxury model cars, much larger and more expensive than their traditional models. These new cars, sold under a different brand, bypassed the VER regulations and allowed them to export more vehicles to the United States.

Honda was the first company to launch a luxury model with its Acura brand. Honda opened sixty Acura dealerships across America in 1986. Acura sales were quick to take off, inspiring Toyota to quickly unveil its Lexus brand in 1989. Nissan's Infiniti arrived that same year. Mazda also planned to launch a luxury line under the brand name Amati, but never did.

Although government export regulations necessitated that these cars be sold under a different brand name, it was really a blessing in disguise for the car companies. These cars were much larger and more luxurious than anything consumers had ever seen from Honda, Toyota, and Nissan. All three brands had established a foothold in the American auto market by creating small, fuel-efficient, and well made cars. Aside from being well made, these new luxury cars were nothing like traditional Japanese vehicles.

It would have been a disaster for Honda to try to convince its customers that they should spend $50,000 on a car with the Honda label on it. That's an impossible mental leap for a consumer conditioned to expect cheap and reliable small cars. The same applies to Toyota and Nissan. Those names just don't stand for *luxury.* Had they attempted to change consumer perceptions, they would have no doubt failed. Yet by placing the luxury cars under a new brand name, all three were extremely successful. Today, Lexus is the market leader in the luxury car sector. By some estimates, the Lexus brand contributes as much as half of the annual US profit for parent company Toyota. In 2009, global brand consultancy Interbrand ranked Lexus as Japan's seventh largest brand, just behind Panasonic.

Meanwhile, General Motors created many of its own problems over the years by watering down what its brands stood for. At one point, each GM brand was designed to be a step up in terms of cost and luxury. But over the years, the lines between a Buick and a Plymouth and an Oldsmobile were blurred. Like many US automakers, GM created standardized platforms on which all of their brands were made, resulting in cars that really weren't that different outside of a nameplate. When GM finally cut loose some of their brands in 2009 and vowed to reestablish their identity, many experts felt it might have come far too late. As GM emerged from bankruptcy protection, it began to make each of its brands unique and powerful by moving to a system where the corporate GM brand would be invisible. Today, the company is attempting to make brands like Buick, Cadillac, and Chevrolet meaningful again by emphasizing those individual brands instead of the GM umbrella.

One multinational company that has been tremendously successful in that regard is Procter & Gamble. P&G has brilliantly created numerous powerful and unique brands under one rather invisible corporate umbrella. They have kept the corporate brand well hidden behind strong brands like Tide, Gillette, Charmin, Crest, and Duracell. All are perceived as world-class brands on their own, not as divisions of Procter & Gamble. The P & G name certainly means something on Wall Street, but nobody goes to the store to buy more Procter & Gamble. Procter & Gamble knows that when it launches a brilliant new product, it isn't the P&G brand name that goes on the main label. Procter & Gamble isn't really a consumer brand at all, but rather a corporate entity that has strategically built individual brands that have generated millions and millions of dollars.

U2 and Procter & Gamble serve as models for how brands can expand and evolve without destroying the equity they have worked hard to acquire with consumers. While the Passengers' album didn't sell nearly as well for U2 as Lexus and Acura sold for Toyota and Honda, it did protect the extremely valuable U2 brand against the erosion and backlash it would have suffered for not living up to customers' expectations.

A BIG UMBRELLA

How large is Procter & Gamble? It is the single largest advertiser on earth, spending more than $8 billion annually. With all that money being spent, have you ever seen an advertisement for Procter & Gamble? You probably can't think of a single one. That's because Procter & Gamble doesn't advertise itself as a brand; it only advertises individual brands. When it creates new products or buys new companies, it creates new brands. Nothing is ever sold as Procter & Gamble. Here are just some of the more widely known brands that Procter & Gamble owns and markets to the world:

- Always (feminine hygiene products)
- Aussie (hair care products)
- Bounty (paper towels)
- Braun (home appliances)
- Cascade (dishwasher detergent)
- Cheer (laundry detergent)
- Crest (toothpaste)
- Charmin (bathroom tissue)
- Dawn (dishwashing detergent)
- Dolce & Gabbana (colognes)
- Downy (fabric softener)
- Duracell (batteries)
- Eukanuba (premium pet food)
- Febreze (deodorizer)
- Gain (detergent)
- Gillette (shaving and bath products)
- Head and Shoulders (shampoo)
- Herbal Essence (hair care products)
- Iams (pet food)
- Ivory (soap)
- Mr. Clean (cleaning products)
- Olay (beauty products)
- Old Spice (colognes and body washes)
- Oral-B (dental products)

- ▶ Pampers (diapers)
- ▶ Pantene (hair care products)
- ▶ Pringles (potato chips)
- ▶ Scope (mouthwash)
- ▶ Tampax (tampons)
- ▶ Tide (laundry detergent)
- ▶ Vicks (cough and cold products)

Look at how many Procter & Gamble brands compete against each other in the same category. Old Spice and Gillette compete for mind share in the men's personal hygiene market. Pantene and Aussie compete in women's hair products. Tide and Gain compete in the laundry room. Iams and Eukanuba compete in the kennel. Procter & Gamble markets unique brands individually, allowing them to compete against one another based on their individual attributes. Eukanuba is a more premium brand than Iams. Old Spice is edgier than Gillette. Each brand has its own place in the consumer's mind, and each is marketed accordingly.

Procter & Gamble does very little visible marketing around its own brand, but instead focuses nearly all of its attention on the many powerful brands under its umbrella. The only advertising you are likely to ever see for Procter & Gamble itself are recruitment ads and materials designed to appeal to investors. Otherwise, the biggest advertiser on the planet devotes all of its resources to supporting its individual brands.

A Rock Star Five-Step Program: Lessons on Brand Extension from U2 and P&G

1. **Know what your fans expect from you.** Talk to them. Open up online dialogue with them. Observe their behavior. How do they use your product? What do they think about your brand?

2. **Never stretch your brand beyond customer expectations.** If you stretch your brand too far beyond these expectations, you'll lose your existing fan base and never gain enough new fans to replace them.

3. **New products need new brands.** Like Honda and Toyota demonstrated with their high-end luxury car models, products that go beyond the expectations of your customers need new brand names. Acura and Lexus would not be around today if they were just extensions of the Honda and Toyota brands. U2 might not be around today if they had released *Original Soundtracks 1* as a U2 album instead of a Passengers album.

4. **Each new brand deserves its own marketing.** P&G doesn't market Old Spice and Ivory Soap together, even though they own both brands and both brands appear in the same bathroom. Honda and Acura are not marketed together. Likewise, U2 and Passengers were never marketed as one.

5. **If you get off track, you can always go back.** When U2 realized that they had drifted away from the expectations of their fans, they went public with their claim to reapply for the job of "best band in the world." They did a pretty good job reapplying, and have continued to rock stadiums night after night.

CHAPTER THREE

▼

BOB MARLEY: JAMMIN' WITH THE BRAND

Great rock stars don't appeal to everybody, especially when they start out. Every band starts out small, playing their music for just a few people in a small bar or coffee shop. Over time, hopefully the buzz grows and the fan base builds, eventually evolving into a stadium full of cheering fans.

The Beatles paid their dues playing clubs in Hamburg, Germany, at all hours of the day and (hard day's) night. They didn't suddenly walk off the plane at JFK into the arms of screaming teenage girls. It took time to perfect their craft, develop a fan base, create some buzz, and build the band into an "overnight sensation."

Even when a band develops into the next big thing, they never really appeal to everybody. It might seem that way when everyone talks about a particular band or when a song hits number one on the charts, but great bands—and great brands—are actually niche oriented. Why do so many brands think they should appeal to everyone? Why do so many brands find it difficult to be disliked by some in order to be loved by others? The irony of this quest to be loved by all is found in the old adage: "If you try to appeal to everybody, you'll end up appealing to nobody." If you build your brand to appeal to everyone, you'll never be the brand that people fall in love with. You'll never be their first choice. You might become the fallback second choice when the brand they love isn't available, but that's about as much as you can hope for.

In product research, there is a dreaded group of respondents called "generic positives." These are the people who say things like "it's okay," "I like it," or "it's my favorite" when they are asked about brands, but they fail to offer any specifics. When some executives see a high generic-positive score, they are often encouraged by the apparent positivity toward their brand. The idea that positive comments can be a negative indication is somewhat difficult to grasp. After all, how can comments like "it's good" and "I like it" be negative?

The problem with generic-positive responses is the lack of specifics. If people can't say exactly why they like you, they probably don't care about you very much. Consider your best friend or your spouse. You could probably name five, ten, or even twenty qualities that you like about him or her. Now consider someone you know casually, someone you neither love nor dislike. Can you name nearly as many specific things you like about that person? Can you name any details that you either like or dislike about him or her? There's a good chance that you can't. You might like that person, but odds are good that if that person disappeared from your life you would hardly notice.

There's a neighborhood restaurant that my family ends up at once every few months. Even though we go out for dinner quite regularly, it is relatively rare that we choose this neighborhood restaurant. It isn't that any of us hate the restaurant. It's not bad, but it's not great. It serves everything and specializes in nothing. It is your typical "club sandwich" restaurant. We usually end up there because our picky family of four can't come to a consensus on where we really want to go. If we were surveyed, we'd all have a generic-positive response about this restaurant. That's not a good thing. Would this restaurant be our first choice for steak? Seafood? Mexican? It wouldn't, even though it serves steak, fish and chips, and quesadillas. It is the place we end up when we can't decide what to do, and that's not a very good foundation for them to build a brand on.

On the other hand, there's a Canadian restaurant chain called Cora. It began as a small diner in Montreal and now has 121 locations across the country. Cora serves only breakfast and lunch. There's no dinner menu, no late-night snacks, and no bar. Cora's menu features only breakfast and lunch items. The menu is stocked with fresh fruit, crepes, pancakes, eggs, and sandwiches. Cora is quite popular, but it closes every day after lunch. Doesn't it stand to reason that if Cora opened for dinner it would do more business?

The answer, as counterintuitive as it may be, is no. Cora does well *because* it only serves breakfast and lunch. When people wonder "where should I go for breakfast?" Cora is likely to come to mind because it has a narrow focus. Cora serves a niche market, and serves it well. And with very few high-profile competitors only serving breakfast and lunch, ownership of the category becomes easier.

In Ries & Trout's 1994 classic *The 22 Immutable Laws of Marketing,* the gurus of positioning state: If you can't be first in a product category, set up a new category you can be first in. If you can't be the dominant leader in a category, establish a new category and own it. Nearly thirty years before Ries & Trout wrote that book, one of the most enduring and popular figures in modern music built a tremendous career on that very law: Robert Nesta Marley.

We know Bob Marley as a reggae singer. In fact, when most people are asked about reggae music, they instantly name Bob Marley. Yet when Marley started singing in 1963, reggae music didn't even have a name. The word "reggae" didn't appear in the Jamaican English dictionary until 1967, when it was listed as a "recently established" word describing ragged and tattered clothing. Trying to pinpoint when the word started to be used to describe music is harder. According to Derrick Morgan, one of the first artists to pioneer the genre, the name came about when producer Bunny Lee created a sound with rhythm guitar and organ that sounded like "reggae, reggae." Musical legend Toots Hibbert suggests that the word evolved from the slang *straggae,* used to describe loose women. He claims that he and some friends were jamming and made up a song based on that word, and they began singing "Do the reggae" instead of "Do the straggae." Meanwhile, Bob Marley offered a more refined version. He claimed that the word evolved from the Latin word *regi,* meaning "to the king." Marley said reggae means "the king's music."

However the word came to be, it is clear that the music was being made before it had a formal name. It was the combination of various forms of traditional island music, brought together by a new generation of musicians like Bob Marley. While it quickly rose in popularity in Jamaica, outside the sun kissed Caribbean, the rest of the world paid little notice. Even into the late 1960s, as Marley's career took off at home and the new "reggae" music grew in popularity across the Antilles, Marley and the music remained unknown outside of the islands.

In 1968, two songs came out that gave the world their first taste of reggae. Johnny Nash had a hit with "Hold Me Tight," and The Beatles gave us "Ob-La-Di, Ob-La-Da," both songs incorporating reggae sounds. Two years later, Paul Simon recorded "Mother and Child Reunion" in Jamaica with Jimmy Cliff's backing band. But another two years would go by until reggae got its big break. In 1974, Eric Clapton hit number one in the United States for the first time with a cover of a Bob Marley song called "I Shot the Sheriff." Suddenly the world started to notice this niche sound and the man most prominently making it.

As reggae grew in popularity, so did Marley. Fans discovered his new music, as well as a back catalog of songs they had never heard before. In the second half of the 1970s, Marley became a major concert draw and a star around the world. Even as Marley's fame grew, he remained true to his reggae roots. Marley rose to a saintly status in Jamaica for his commitment to the Jamaican culture, Rastafarianism, and social justice. Marley could have compromised these values to try to become a bigger star. He could have recorded a disco song or done a duet with a big female star of the day. But he didn't. He stayed true to his reggae music niche and that's part of the reason he became so iconic.

Photo credit: Photofest

Bob Marley performing live in 1980.

You become successful by appealing passionately to a small group of people for very specific reasons. You will alienate some people in the process, but great brands accept that risk. Southwest Airlines became the largest airline in the United States by creating a new product category, low-cost airline, of which they became the clear-cut leader. When they took off for the first time, there were no low-cost airlines. There were simply airlines, vying to be the leader of a very generic category. Southwest dominates the entire industry by leading a very specific category. Rock star brands run from the generic.

It sounds like a contradiction that to be successful, you have to avoid trying to appeal to everyone. Find something that nobody else is doing, and do it well. Resist the temptation to change what you do so you can appeal to more people. Embrace the fact that if you are doing something interesting, some people will not like you.

As Roy H. Williams, author of the popular trilogy *The Wizard of Ads*, said, "The risk of insult is the price of clarity." Imagine what a disaster it would have been for Marley to record a disco song in the late 1970s simply to appeal to the mass audience! His true fans in Jamaica would never have accepted it. The people who love Marley for his reggae music would have abandoned him because he no longer would have represented what they thought he stood for.

You see that kind of misguided thinking every day with major brands.

Fried chicken is hardly a small niche, but it is a niche within the fast-food market. And for many years Kentucky Fried Chicken filled that niche brilliantly. But as diners started to become more health conscious, Kentucky Fried Chicken couldn't resist the chance to appeal to health nuts by offering up grilled chicken and an extensive menu of salads. Kentucky Fried Chicken has the word "fried" in its name! It isn't about *grilled* chicken; it's about *fried* chicken! To help get away from the stigma of fried chicken, Kentucky Fried Chicken changed its name to the acronym KFC. Although the grilled chicken initially sold well, it left a bad taste in the mouths of a coalition of franchisees who banded together in 2010 to sue the company for taking the focus away from fried chicken.

Although it took a few years, KFC's focus on health appears to have abated somewhat. KFC still carries grilled chicken and salads, but the focus has shifted to products like the new "Double Down," a now legendary, calorie-rich sandwich made from two pieces of fried chicken, cheese, and bacon instead of bread. The Double Down quickly took off after its launch on April 12, 2010. By June, KFC had cooked up 10 million of the artery-clogging sandwiches to the tune of $50 million in revenue! According to analysts, that figure represents 5 percent of the company's sales in that time period.

The Double Down was successful because it is a niche product in a niche category. It doesn't appeal to everyone. It serves the fried chicken niche perfectly. It allows KFC to celebrate its niche, not run from it and hide behind healthy foods. What kind of state is a brand in when it is ashamed of what it makes? In a health-conscious world, an unhealthy treat is a niche worth exploiting.

Jeep is a brand that fills a niche, but these days even Jeep is having a hard time resisting the chance to appeal to more urban buyers who want a fuel-efficient car with a Jeep label. So Jeep created the Jeep Compass. Up until the arrival of the Compass and the Liberty, all Jeep vehicles were "trail rated." Every Jeep that rolled off the assembly line was certified to take on the famous Rubicon Trail in California's Sierra Nevada mountain range. This created Jeep's rugged reputation. Sure, the vehicles were hard on fuel. You don't get to take on the Rubicon Trail *and* get forty miles to the gallon! They were built for the army in World War II, and they were built to take bullets. It takes gas to power a vehicle that tough. So what happens when Jeep takes off that trail-rated badge and creates a line of car-like SUVs that get better gas mileage, aren't four wheel drive, and are made for the paved roads of the city? The brand stops being an intriguing niche and gets watered down.

Bloomberg Businessweek called Jeep's Compass "misguided," and sales quickly dropped from a high of just more than 39,000 in 2007 to less than 16,000 in 2010. For 2011, Jeep redesigned the Compass and attempted to position it alongside the luxurious Grand Cherokee using the tagline "A grand new jeep." No matter what impact this might have on sales, the Compass dilutes the Jeep brand, and the more watered-down the brand gets, the less value it has. Jeep is treading on dangerous territory. Even if this strategy results in short-term sales, it will come at great expense to the brand itself.

Bob Marley was a niche artist. He never faltered from his niche. His fan base grew because of what he truly was, not because of what he tried to be to please them. Even thirty years after his death, Marley's estate continues to earn an estimated $9 million a year, and his catalog of reggae music is worth more than $100 million. That's one profitable niche brand.

NICHE BRANDING CASE STUDY: JONES SODA

For niche player Jones Soda, the biggest obstacles have come when it ventured away from its niche base and attempted to compete head-to-head with the big mainstream boys.

Jones Soda was introduced in 1996, and in a few short years, it established a reputation for quirky and interesting flavors with just as quirky artwork on its bottles. Jones Soda wasn't like Coke and Pepsi. It was different, with black and white photographs and catchy phrases on the bottles. Jones Soda proudly rolled out goofy flavors like FuFu Berry, Fun, and Happy alongside traditional root beer, cola, and cream soda. Instead of attempting to sell its product in convenience and grocery stores like the big guys, Jones Soda placed its product in music stores, clothing stores, sporting goods retailers, and tattoo shops. These venues attracted a specific, young consumer that Jones Soda knew would become fans of its product. Over time, Jones Soda worked its way into 7-Eleven, Safeway, and other major stores.

Doing the crazy things that the Cokes and Pepsis couldn't do—such as unveiling themed flavors that became collector's items—made Jones Soda a household name. In

2003, Jones Soda released "Turkey and Gravy" to celebrate Thanksgiving, and it quickly sold out. The following year the soda company assembled an entire drinkable Thanksgiving meal, featuring "Turkey and Gravy" along with "Mashed Potatoes and Butter," "Cranberry," and "Green Bean Casserole." The gift pack was so sought after that the company's website temporarily crashed as people attempted to buy them online. People were paying $100 for the collection on eBay!

Creating unusual flavors wasn't the only way that Jones Soda went against the major players. While Coke and Pepsi sweeten their drinks with high-fructose corn syrup, Jones Soda rejected it in 2007 in favor of using all-natural cane sugar instead. While Coke and Pepsi had standard labels, Jones Soda invited customers to contribute photographs to be used on the soda bottles. Customers can even order personalized "my Jones Soda" bottles featuring their own photographs and sayings.

So why did Jones Soda need to lay off 40 percent of its workforce in 2008?

Jones Soda ran into trouble when it attempted to compete directly with Coke and Pepsi by straying from glass bottles and using cans. It didn't work out so well. As soon as Jones Soda stopped playing like a niche player and started playing by the big guy's rules, it became less successful. Attempts to become the official soda of Starbucks, Alaska Airlines, and the Seattle Seahawks have all started with good intentions and eventually fallen apart because Jones Soda *isn't* a mainstream product. When it attempts to position itself as a competitor to Coke and Pepsi, Jones Soda inevitably fails. However, when it positions itself as an unusual niche player, Jones Soda succeeds brilliantly.

Recently, Jones Soda executives contemplated selling the company at a dramatic discount but backed out of the deal at the last minute. A new CEO was named, one with experience in niche beverage markets. There is hope for the future of Jones Soda, as long as it remains passionately focused on being a niche brand.

A Rock Star Five-Step Program: Legendary Brands That Created New Product Categories

Bob Marley didn't become the world's top-selling musician, he became the world's top-selling *reggae* musician. He owned an entirely new product category. Here are five brands that created entirely new product categories instead of trying to conquer existing mountains. You'll probably notice that most of these niche brands not only dominate their own unique product categories, but they also do extremely well in broader product categories.

1. **Quizno's.** Instead of taking on Subway, the dominant leader in sandwich shops, Quizno's created the toasted sub and instantly became the leader in that new category. Subway was forced to add toasted subs to its menu, but Quizno's had already staked out that territory. Their positioning statement, "Mmmm Toasty," reinforces their category.

2. **Red Bull.** Competing with Pepsi and Coke in the "cola" category wasn't a smart option, nor was taking on Gatorade in the "sports drink" category. Red Bull instead created the "energy drink" category. Their unique taste, ingredients, and even can size defined the difference. Red Bull continues to dominate the energy drink category despite immense competition.

3. **iPad.** After years of building a strong number two brand in personal computers, Apple surged ahead into the leadership role in the tablet computer market with its wildly successful iPad in 2010. The release of the iPad 2 in

continued on following page

2011 put Apple in a position where no other competitors are likely to catch up anytime soon. Apple still doesn't dominate personal computers, but they dominate tablet computers by a wide margin.

4. **Chipotle Mexican Grill.** The fastest-growing fast-food chain in America is a leader in the new product category of "responsible and sustainable fast food." The Mexican food category was already extremely crowded, but by creating a policy of "food with integrity" and using organic, local, and free-range products, Chipotle created and owned this new category. Because they created a new product category, Chipotle doesn't really have to worry as much about Taco Bell, Qdoba, Rubio's, or Baja Fresh.

5. **Southwest Airlines.** The most famous example of creating a new product category is Southwest Airlines. Today they are the number one passenger airline in the United States, but they got there by being the leading low-cost carrier. That product category didn't exist until Southwest came along and created it. By creating a new category, they carved out a profitable niche that led to the eventual dominance of the entire industry.

▼

CHAPTER FOUR

DEAD HEADS AND PARROT HEADS: BUILDING A TRIBE

He's only really had one hit. It was a simple little beach song from 1977 about living on the beach, contemplating life, and wondering who was to blame for his present situation.

For decades fans have been singing along to "Margaritaville" night after night at Jimmy Buffett concerts. Buffett remains one of the top concert draws in the world! Every concert brings fans together from thousands of miles away, as they plan vacations around his tour dates and celebrate each concert as if it were a dysfunctional family reunion. Buffett is one of music's richest stars and most powerful brands. His name is on the growing chain of Margarita-ville restaurants in the Caribbean and North America, and hotels, casinos, a line of clothing, footwear, blenders, beer, tequila, and books. Not surprisingly, his brand also includes music. Mailboat Records distributes both Buffett's own music and other artists who share a vision similar to his. The Margaritaville brand is even strong enough to support a satellite radio channel that plays music with an acoustic/beach feel from a wide range of rock, country, and folk artists.

Who is responsible for this empire? Certainly Buffett is a smart and very hardworking businessman surrounded by bright advisors, but you can thank the Parrot Heads for a big part of it.

Since early in his career, Buffett has attracted and nurtured a community of fans who embraced his music and beach-bum lifestyle. But things really took off when he decided to give up some of the control and let his fans drive the boat forward. For many years before the formal formation of the Parrot Heads Club, fans had been tailgating before each Buffett show, fueled by margaritas, beer, and sunshine. It wasn't an organized thing, just a gathering of people who wanted to create their own little Margaritaville for a few hours. The tailgate parties included limbo contests, body painting, vibrator races, margarita-making contests, and plenty of tropical costumes and risqué drunken fun. For adults working a nine-to-five grind five days a week, a Buffett concert became an escape from reality and a chance to spend a few hours living on a tropical beach and strumming a guitar.

As Buffett made his way across the country each summer, the legend of both the concert and the tailgate parties grew, and fans in greater and greater numbers started making a Buffett concert the central party of their summer. During a mid-1980s tour stop in Cincinnati, Ohio, Buffett guitarist Timothy B. Schmit dubbed the growing number of Hawaiian-shirt and flip-flop wearing fans "Parrot Heads," adopting the term from the famous Grateful Dead fans, the Dead Heads.

Buffett already had an official fan club where members received periodic mailings called "The Coconut Telegraph" that shared stories about Buffett and where he was playing live. What Buffett was doing with his fan club was not unusual. In the 1970s and 1980s, most artists had developed some sort of mailing list, but what transpired in 1989 changed everything.

A certain fan named Scott Nickerson decided to bring together some of the great people he had met tailgating at Buffett concerts in his hometown of Atlanta. His idea was that this group would meet for drinks and talk all-things tropical. Since Buffett usually played in town only once a year, these little gatherings would provide another chance to get together. Nickerson also figured that they could give something back by doing some goodwill work in the community. To advertise the planned get together, he took out a small ad in the local entertainment newsletter. On April 1, 1989, Scott's group of fifteen Parrot Heads met for the first time. Each time the group would get together, friends would bring friends and more and more people would show up to savor margaritas, share stories, connect with like-minded people, and give something back to charities and causes in their city.

Nickerson found his little Parrot Head club growing quickly and figured the concept would work in other cities just as well as it was taking hold in Atlanta. So he decided to bring the idea to Buffett himself. Nickerson contacted Buffett's attorneys to make sure he wasn't violating any trademarks and found in them a surprising ally. Instead of trying to shut down Nickerson's group, they helped him get it rolling. They spelled out clearly what Buffett trademarks they could and couldn't use, and they supported Nickerson in his efforts to spread the idea.

Soon after, a short article about the Atlanta Parrot Head club appeared in an edition of Buffett's newsletter, "The Coconut Telegraph." As soon as that mailing went out to the official fan club, Nickerson was swamped with requests from fans asking how they could start their own local Parrot Head club. Parrot Heads in Paradise Inc. was born.

There was no involvement from Buffett or his lawyers. They didn't do any work to build it or to fuel the fire. The fans did the work. Nickerson wrote the official guidelines, and they still stand today. He helped organize Parrot Head clubs in several states that first year, as well as the first-ever "Meeting of the Minds" Parrot Head convention in 1992 at the Margaritaville Café in New Orleans. It was a tremendous success. Each year, membership in the Parrot Heads in Paradise and attendance at the "Meeting of the Minds" grew and grew. In 1998, more than 2,000 Parrot Heads descended on Key West, Florida, for the 7th annual event, and Jimmy himself appeared in person and played live for more than an hour. Since then, Buffet and his band have turned up unannounced more than a few times to perform at no charge for the Parrot Heads in Paradise convention.

Today, Nickerson continues to work with the organization as they administer more than 200 official clubs in the United States, Canada, and the Caribbean. The group is a registered non-profit organization and in 2009 they raised more than $2.8 million for local and national charities. They are clear that while they are a group of people who are Buffett fans, they are not a fan club. Their mission goes far beyond simply promoting Buffett's music. For Buffett, the wonderful benefit of having the Parrot Heads in Paradise movement on his side is that it has created a built-in network of fans for each stop on the Buffett tour. The thousands of Parrot Heads not only buy tickets themselves, but they also act as ambassadors and bring their friends along and introduce them to the brand.

What makes Buffett unusual is that he embraced the idea of giving up some control over his brand, allowing his fans to run with their idea. Buffett's lawyers could have put a quick demise to Nickerson's Parrot Heads in Paradise idea. After all, Buffett already had an official fan club. Nickerson's group didn't have any legal right to use his name or adapt his brand for their benefit. Many artists would have shut down this kind of club for fear that the fans might say or do something contrary to the artist's official position. Lawyers, sadly, don't always see the benefit to this sort of thing. Fortunately,

Buffett saw an opportunity. He realized that if he gave up control and let the fans take ownership of it, the movement would become bigger than anything he could create himself. When fans talk to other fans, something magical happens. Magic definitely took hold, turning the Parrot Heads in Paradise from a one-chapter group into an international phenomenon.

Letting fans set the agenda and losing some control over his brand made perfect sense. It created a fantastic word-of-mouth sensation because conversations between fans are far more powerful than advertising messages. When friends talk, there are no secrets or suspicions between people like there are with traditional marketing messages. Fan-to-fan marketing facilitated an organic wildfire that spread the Buffett brand better than any advertisements could have.

Were there risks? Absolutely. Jimmy Buffett had to keep his legal distance, making sure that he absolved himself from the activities of the group in the event that something seriously bad were to happen. After all, someone could have been hurt or killed at one of their events. They could have done damage to Buffett's reputation. Plenty of bad things could have happened, but the benefits clearly outweighed the risks. The Buffett brand is an incredible empire today, across many connected platforms.

What makes the Buffett brand so much more powerful than most music brands? According to Scott Nickerson, the passion among his fans has a lot to do with how different Buffett is. While most artists sing songs about a wide variety of topics, Buffett's songs tend to focus on his beach-bum lifestyle. Certainly the songs range in topic from love songs to drinking songs, but all of them come back to the central theme of living the carefree life on a tropical beach. Nickerson's observation, having witnessed the growth of the brand from a front-row seat, is that Buffett has a special kind of fan.

Jimmy Buffett's beach-bum lifestyle was always reflected in his music.

"Parrot Heads will go to show after show after show, all summer," Nickerson said. "They have the money and they love the experience and they'll see every show they can. His fans are possessed!"

That level of passion among fans has allowed Buffett to build a wildly successful brand that goes far beyond music.

Wisely though, every aspect of Buffett's vast empire is connected back to what his brand stands for. While his name may be on things as disconnected as hamburgers, shoes, and books, all are connected by the tropical lifestyle theme.

So just how far does the Jimmy Buffett brand extend?

His chain of Margaritaville Cafés, casinos, and hotels has expanded from Key West and the Caribbean to places like Niagara Falls, Chicago, Calgary, and Nashville. The Margaritaville Hotel opened in 2010 in Pensacola Beach, Florida. Meanwhile in Biloxi, Mississippi, plans are in place to build the Margaritaville Casino and Restaurant in the city's back bay. The Cheeseburger in Paradise restaurant chain began in Indiana, and has expanded to thirty-four locations across America. Buffett licenses the "Cheeseburger in Paradise" name to OSI Restaurants, owners of Outback Steakhouse, and they run the restaurants.

Land Shark Bar and Grill is a new concept restaurant scheduled to open in Myrtle Beach, South Carolina, already home to a Margaritaville Café. Jimmy Buffett's at the Beachcomber puts Buffett's mark on Hawaii with this themed restaurant and bar in Waikiki. And it wouldn't be the Buffett experience without a full retail store attached, would it?

Land Shark Lager beer is a Buffett brand brewed in a cooperative venture with Anheuser-Busch. To promote the beer, Jimmy signed a one-year deal to rename the home stadium of the Miami Dolphins as Land Shark Stadium for the 2009 football season.

Buffett's passion for baseball brought his brand into

franchise ownership with the Fort Myers Miracle and Madison Black Wolf. He co-owns the Fort Myers team with actor Bill Murray, although the Madison team has since folded.

The Margaritaville Cargo Store is an online store, although it also sells products in selected retail outlets in North America. The "Frozen Concoction Maker" sells at a price that puts a normal blender to shame. The "Fiji" model, one of six variations on the market, retails for $350. You can also pick up accessories for the party, such as Margaritaville-branded party coolers and tailgating grills. Margaritaville Lifestyle (clothing and footwear) sells online and at the twelve retail stores attached to Margaritaville Cafés. Merchandise and clothing apparently attract as many people as the food does! The T-shirts are hugely popular, but selling flip-flops and boat shoes to wannabe pirates is also a big business.

Mailboat Records doesn't only distribute Jimmy's music. It also supports a number of artists both new and old who make music in the same vein as Buffett. Those artists often get played on Radio Margaritaville, a station on XM/Sirius satellite radio. The station also plays other artists and often features concert playbacks from Buffett shows.

Buffett has authored several books, both fiction and non-fiction. His most recent book, *Swine Not*, came out in 2008. All of Buffett's books are centered on unusual characters and captivating stories that come from his tropical experiences.

The entire empire owes a tremendous debt to the Parrot Heads, who stop at nothing to express their love for the music and their passion for the beach-bum lifestyle. Scott Nickerson remains amazed by the fanaticism, saying that the only other fans who even come close are the world-famous Dead Heads, from whom they drew their name.

The Grateful Dead themselves represent a tribe-building example like no other act in rock 'n' roll history.

The Dead became one of the most successful live bands in the world thanks to authentic, word-of-mouth marketing generated almost entirely by their fans. It wasn't radio airplay—they had almost none. It wasn't hype or advertising—there wasn't any of that either. The Grateful Dead built their initial fan base night after night, jamming for hours in stadiums and arenas. They developed a reputation for their long sets, improvisation, and stellar musicianship. The Grateful Dead rose as leaders in the late 1960s, West Coast hippie counterculture. But the true establishment of the tribe of fanatical followers known as Dead Heads began with a simple note inside the album *Grateful Dead* in 1971. It read:

> *DEAD FREAKS UNITE: Who are you? Where are you? How are you? Send us your name and address and we'll keep you informed. Dead Heads, P.O. Box 1065, San Rafael, California 94901.*

And that's how the movement began to organize, turning fans of a band into a connected tribe. They were at first driven primarily by a common passion for the band's music, but it quickly developed into a lifestyle organization, committed to common values and ideals. The group formed their own idioms and slang. Along the way, numerous sub-groups developed within the group based on tenure, sobriety (Wharf Rats), religion (Jews for Jerry), lifestyle (Rainbow Tribe), and level of devotion (Spinners).

The Dead Head movement wasn't something the band worked hard to build. They simply connected their fans to the band and to each other. Certainly the explosion of Dead Heads was fueled by the way the band went against the grain of the music industry and actively supported the bootlegging of their shows. In fact, the taping of Dead shows became so popular that in 1984 the Grateful Dead actually created sections in the crowd where tapers could get the best possible audio recording of the concert. The only stipulation that the band and the tapers themselves put on the recordings was that they be freely shared, with no money ever changing hands. Incredibly, it has become strict custom within the Dead Head community to freely share the music in the tradition of the original tapers. That sharing became the foundation for the growth of the Dead Heads. Fans shared with each other, expanding the band's reach without their active involvement.

This dedication to freely sharing led to millions of people being exposed to music that they otherwise would have never heard. Fans of the band shared their discovery with their friends, spreading the band's following one fan at a time. Did the Grateful Dead lose out on potential album sales because they allowed their live shows to be taped? If they did, it was only in the short term. In the long run, fans wanted to hear the music in all of its forms, live and in-studio, and they wanted to support the band. The Grateful Dead sold millions of albums precisely *because* they allowed their live shows to be taped and shared. They sold millions more concert tickets because people had heard bootlegs of their live shows and felt the need to experience it in person. How is that for counterintuitive?

The band could afford to let their recorded music be shared freely because their business model was built on ticket sales for live shows, not revenue driven by album sales and the record company "system." With millions of self-declared Dead Heads following the band religiously, they were virtually guaranteed sell-out crowds night after night in every city where they performed. And true Dead Heads came back every night because the band played a different set list each night. While most live bands played the same set list in Phoenix as they did in Philadelphia and Portland, The Dead created a unique experience every night, changing the set list and the vibe of the evening. That made every concert worth buying tickets for, even if you had seen the band dozens of times already. And because every show was taped and shared, being at a truly special show where the band was exceptionally tight or the set list was indelibly unique became a Dead Head badge of honor. As tapes of these famous epic Dead shows circulated, fans who were there could boast about having seen in person the 1973 "Watkins Jam" or the legendary June 1970 show at the Capitol Theatre in Port Chester, NY.

It is vital to once again reiterate that the band didn't actively do much to facilitate the growth of the Dead Heads phenomenon. They didn't set out to build a fan club per se. They simply connected people to the band and to each other. It isn't what they did that stands out as a lesson in building a rock star brand. It's what they *didn't* do that matters:

- They didn't try to stop people from recording their concerts.

- They didn't sue people for trading copies of the band's live shows.

- They didn't stop people from selling their homemade clothing, jewelry, or food along "Shakedown Street" outside the venue.

- They didn't try to eliminate recordings of their weaker shows. The band was the band, warts and all.

By not getting in the way of their fans' passion, the Grateful Dead and Jimmy Buffett both created massive networks of passionate people to help spread the message about their music. Incredibly, all of this happened before the rise of the Internet and social networking sites such as Facebook and Twitter. Imagine how fast the Dead Head and Parrot Head viruses could have spread through the power of technology! That's the opportunity brands have today if they are willing to lose some control and let the fans take over and own their experience.

Who maintains your brand's Facebook profile? Most likely, if your brand has a Facebook profile, it is maintained by someone in your company. Most brands use their Facebook profile to spread their corporate message, simply interpreting social media as another advertising venue. What would happen if you turned the administration of your Facebook profile over to some of your biggest fans? Would the message change? Instead of corporate press releases, your Facebook wall would be full of real-life comments about your brand and how it impacts the lives of the people who use it. Instead of a one-way advertising tool, it could become a two-way communication street. Is it risky? Sure it is, but what smart move doesn't carry some risk?

It may soon come to be that creating a customer-driven brand is impossible to avoid. You may either have to surrender some control over your brand or risk becoming obsolete. That's because today's marketers are speaking to a generation raised on a personalized experience. The very kids who a decade ago created their own teddy bear at Build-A-Bear are now buying cars and appliances. These are the children who created entire communities on the computer game *The Sims* that were completely unique to them. These consumers won't settle for anything less than brands that are responsive to them. Allowing these new consumers to take some control over your brand will give them the chance to create a customized experience and deepen the bond between the brand and the customer.

A Rock Star Five-Step Program: Five Keys to Social Media Success

Jimmy Buffett and the Grateful Dead are two of the best examples of musical acts who have established massive fan networks, and they did so without the benefit of the numerous social media tools that exist today. If you want to build a successful network of fans for your brand, there's no doubt that social media will play a role. Entire books are dedicated to how to use social media to advance your business, but here are a few key points to consider as you embark on a social media strategy:

1. **Have a conversation.** You aren't broadcasting your advertising message to people. Social media is a dialogue, a two-way street. Rock star brands use social media as much to hear from their customers as they do to send messages to them.

2. **Listen carefully.** People are talking about your brand and they are using Facebook and Twitter to do it. Rock star brands monitor the social media channels and observe what is being said about them. Often they can prevent negatives from spreading by addressing customer concerns quickly.

3. **Be authentic.** Fans of Twitter celebrities like Lady Gaga and Justin Bieber see Twitter as a chance to hear directly from their idols. Charlie Sheen has used social media to show his true colors. Social media isn't a place to put on a fake front; it is a place to be real and honest.

4. **Encourage feedback.** Ask your customers to tell you what they think. Involve them. Coke partnered with rock band

continued on following page

Maroon 5 in March 2011 and invited fans to be in the studio to provide input on the creation of a song. The twenty-four-hour session resulted in a song that fans took a personal stake in because they were asked to provide feedback.

5. **Interact frequently.** Jimmy Buffett and the Grateful Dead didn't establish these huge fan networks and then ignore them. Continue to develop conversations, share information, and talk to your customers. Become friends. Build trust. Don't expect your social network to flourish without frequent updates and constant attention.

▼

CHAPTER FIVE

ARE YOU EXPERIENCED?

The world didn't listen to Jimi Hendrix; they experienced Jimi Hendrix. Watching him on stage coaxing the fire from his guitar was an experience. *Are You Experienced* was arguably his most famous album. His band was even called "the Experience." Sadly, we experienced far too little of Hendrix. He died in September 1970, two months shy of his twenty-eighth birthday.

"Experience" is a vital word for brands, and not nearly enough brands understand that. No matter what you sell, it is all about the experience: the emotional reaction that your customers have when they use your brand. Rock star brands realize that they don't sell products or services, they sell experiences. Products and services are easily duplicated, boring, and of little value. Experiences are one-of-a-kind, exciting, and extremely valuable.

More than one million motorcycles are sold every year in the United States alone. Certainly driving a motorcycle on the open road is an experience, but does the experience really change if you alter the brand of the cycle? It shouldn't, but Harley-Davidson would like you to think so.

Harley-Davidson doesn't sell motorcycles. Harley-Davidson sells the ability for a forty-seven-year-old accountant to dress up in black leather, ride through small towns, and have people be afraid of him. It's an experience that Harley calls the "rebel lifestyle." It sells that experience not only through motorcycles but also through a wealth of merchandise and accessories. Almost 5 percent of Harley-Davidson's annual revenues come from licensing their logo for clothing and other non-motorcycle related items.

The average Harley-Davidson customer isn't, by profile, much of a rebel. The median age of a Harley customer is 46.7 years old with a household income of $83,000, nearly double the national average. The reality is that hardcore, anti-establishment rebels don't make $83,000 a year, and because of that fact selling high-end motorcycles to them is a losing proposition. Harley-Davidson customers are relatively wealthy people who want to buy into the rebel experience, they are not criminally inclined highway pirates.

Starbucks doesn't actually sell coffee. Starbucks sells the experience of relaxing in a quiet place where you can escape the real world for a few minutes or a few hours to read, relax, chat, and enjoy a drink. Starbucks sells the experience of savoring a higher quality cup of coffee through beverages and food as well as through the décor, wi-fi, and in-store music. Even the words that Starbucks uses to describe the sizes of their coffee—tall, grande, and venti—are part of the experience. Many people love Starbucks coffee and swear by it, but the Starbucks' experience is about so much more than that. When you walk out of the store carrying your to-go cup of Starbucks coffee, you are sending a message to others about your tastes. That's part of the Starbucks' experience.

Guinness doesn't sell beer. Guinness sells the experience of getting together with friends and sharing stories and laughing, just like they have been doing at Irish pubs for centuries. When you sip on a pint of deep, dark Guinness, you are stepping into that pub and soaking in hundreds of years of brewing tradition. You are telling others that you are refined and above "bowling-alley beer."

The idea that Guinness is more than just another beer is reinforced by Guinness itself through its explicit instructions on how the beer should be stored, served, and poured. According to the company, it should take exactly 119.53 seconds to pour the perfect pint of draught Guinness. That lengthy pour has become central to the brand's marketing message, "Good things come to those who wait." Their award-winning marketing includes a famous 1999 commercial called "Surfer" that was named "Best Ad of All Time" in a 2002 poll in the British newspaper *Sunday Times*. The commercial features a group of surfers who wait patiently for the perfect wave. They wait and wait until finally the perfect wave arrives, proving the Guinness slogan is true: "Good things come to those who wait."

Almost any product can serve as an example of how the experience matters more than the product or service. Nobody wakes up and craves Crest or Colgate. They crave clean, white teeth and fresh breath that makes them attractive to others. It isn't the quarter-inch drill bit that people crave, it is the desire to hang pictures and do home improvements. We don't buy products; we buy the benefit of the product. We buy into the experience. That's what motivates us to buy.

Rock star brands sell benefits. They sell experiences. They sell temporary escapes from real life. Music is no different, and songs are the ultimate escape.

Bruce Springsteen sells a visit to small town America where working-class values like hard work and honesty prevail against corporate greed and evil. Springsteen can play for 20,000 people at Madison Square Garden and make you feel like you've walked into a depressed Pennsylvania mining town when he sings "The River."

In the 1970s, KISS sold kids the chance to walk into a fire-breathing, blood-spitting dark comic-book circus. Their look, sound, and intense live show made them a parent's nightmare, which only served to contribute to the experience for the youth. Going to a KISS concert was a true experience. When you got home, there was still homework to do and chores to look after, so you couldn't actually "rock and roll all night and party every day." But while you were at the concert, you really believed you could.

Rock star brands spend very little time talking about their actual product. They spend the majority of their time talking about how the brand makes you feel and what benefit it brings to your life.

Do you really know what experience your brand provides?

Think about cars. BMW's experience is performance. Volvo's experience is safety. Jeep's experience is rugged. Prius's experience is being environmentally friendly. Each car maker knows how to satisfy its customers' needs. They know what experience they provide. While every one of those cars will get you from home to work and back, each car will make your drive to work a different experience.

You don't need to be a multibillion dollar automaker to understand what experience you provide to your customers. Consider the case of two local hometown plumbers. One advertises the experience of doing bathroom renovations that stun people. His company uses the absolute best quality fixtures, and the work his company does is the sort of thing you see in magazines. He turns bathrooms into spas. The other company advertises the experience of comfort, knowing you weren't ripped off when you had your repairs done. His company's advertising talks about honesty, fairness, and value.

Which plumber will you call when you want to do a $10,000 bathroom renovation?

Which plumber will get the call when you need someone to fix a perpetually dripping faucet?

Each plumber has wisely created a different customer experience. So what happens to the third plumber whose advertisement says "for all of your plumbing needs"? He doesn't get any calls because nobody wants to experience the generic. Brands that solve generic problems inevitably fail because people don't *have* generic problems. We have specific problems. People have very specific problems and want very unique and specific experiences.

The best way to fully understand what experience you provide is to do basic customer research. Talk to your fans in person and online. Observe the conversations they are having online about your brand. What words do your customers use to describe how they feel when they use your brand? Forget about what you *think* they think about you. Forget about what you think about yourself. Instead, focus on the words and phrases they use to describe your brand, their interaction with it, and how they describe competing brands. Why do they choose you (or them)? Most often you'll need to look beyond the tangible things like price, although saving money can be an amazing customer experience . . . just ask Walmart.

Walmart has built a massive brand based on the idea that they can save you money on just about any product. Customers revel in it. But for most brands, winning the battle to be cheapest is a difficult one. There is almost always someone who can make a competing product cheaper. Generally your brand will need to provide a different experience than just being the cheapest option in order to win, for example:

- ▶ Do you make your customer's life easier like Staples?

- ▶ Do you make your customer feel safe and secure like ADT Home Security?

- ▶ Do you make your customer feel special and loved like Tiffany & Co.?

- ▶ Do you make your customer feel cutting-edge and cool like Apple?

When you discover your brand's experience—how you make your customer feel—you'll discover a wealth of new ways to promote your brand and connect on a deeper level with your customers.

MARKETING AND BRAIN LATERALIZATION

Rock star brands that sell experiences instead of products understand the concept of brain lateralization. Simply put, the human brain is divided into two connected hemispheres. The left side of the brain is the accountant, handling things like exact mathematical calculations, literal language interpretation, and fact retrieval. The right side of the brain is the artist, dealing with estimated and approximated calculations, interpretive language understanding like nuances and facial expressions, and contextual meanings. While the two hemispheres of the brain work together at all times, most scientists believe that each individual has a more dominant side of the brain. Those who prefer thinking with their left brain look for facts and logic, statistics and figures, and supporting evidence. Right brain thinkers want to hear emotional stories, allegories and metaphors, and artistic expressions.

One of the challenges in marketing to the left brain is that it is extremely judgmental and logical. It can be difficult to persuade the left brain to take action when it doesn't view an advertisement as pragmatic. Why buy a $25,000 Harley-Davidson when the left brain says you can get just as good a motorcycle for $15,000 with a different name on it? Certainly a left-brain thinker would look at the price tag and the specs and buy the cheaper bike.

That's why selling the experience makes so much sense. When you sell your experience and not your product, you leave the logical left brain behind and enter the brain through the free-thinking right side. Selling the experience is like a free pass into the brain!

Let's look at that $25,000 Harley-Davidson purchase. Selling it to the left brain is nearly impossible. You could make the case that the product is better, but is it *that* much better? Is it so much better that the left brain is going to rubber stamp an extra $10,000 price tag? It simply isn't going to happen. If the buying decision is based entirely on left-brain logic, the Harley-Davidson bike is going to sit on the lot until the end of time. But when the Harley *experience* is presented, the right brain takes over. It is in the realm of the right brain where stories are heard and interpreted. The right brain is where we see ourselves wrapping our legs around that roaring engine, revving it up, and hitting the road sneering at anyone who doesn't have a Harley-Davidson logo on their bike.

In an entirely left-brain world, we wouldn't go to the movies because it would be impossible to suspend reality for ninety minutes to appreciate a story, let alone deal with the price of a movie ticket when loads of movies are playing at home on Netflix. At sporting events we would never cheer for the underdog in the big game because statistics would tell us who is likely to win.

If the left brain ruled the world, would classic brands like Tiffany & Co., Harley-Davidson, and Guinness even exist?

A Rock Star Five-Step Program: Finding Your "Experience"

The idea of selling your experience, not your product, seems easy enough. But when you actually sit down to determine what your brand's true experience is, the whole process gets complicated. Each of your customers is different, and each might find a different use for your brand. Here are five things to consider when determining how consumers experience your brand:

1. **What problem do you solve?** Regardless of what you sell, people are buying your product because you solve some sort of problem they have.

2. **Think geographically.** Your experience could be that you are the local alternative to a global brand, and that's perfectly fine.

3. **Consider your customer's motivations.** We all have ideal visions of ourselves that we strive for. Market your product to those ideals. There are plenty of people ordering a Big Mac and Diet Coke because they want to watch their weight.

4. **Examine your competitors.** What problem do they solve? Now, look at how you solve it differently, such as Lowe's offering a more collaborative and less intimidating alternative to Home Depot.

5. **Monitor what your customers are saying about your brand online.** Observe the conversations and attempt to reflect those conversations in your marketing. It is so much easier to persuade people of something they already believe than it is to try and change their minds.

▼

CHAPTER SIX

THE BRANDING EQUATION: DEMAND + SCARCITY = VALUE

Hanover Street connects downtown Boston to the historic North End, running straight through the heart of Paul Revere's old neighborhood. Over the decades, dominance of the North End has changed from the Irish to the Jewish to today's "Little Italy." On a warm sunny day, it seems like half of New England is here soaking up the history and enjoying the atmosphere. Along Hanover Street are numerous wonderful pastry shops known for their cannoli, a Sicilian treat made of a tube of fried pastry dough filled with a creamy ricotta cheese-based filling. You can get cannoli at nearly every pastry shop in the North End, but if you want cannoli from Mike's Pastry, you'll need to wait in line. I've done so many times, and I've never regretted it.

Yet many locals will tell you with good authority that the cannoli down the street at Modern Pastry is just as good, and maybe better some say. Nearby Caffe Graffiti will sell you a cannoli that's just as good. And some say Caffe Vittoria makes a cannoli that's even better, and they serve it to you in a nicer environment. As the line gets longer at Mike's Pastry, the other pastry shop owners stand and watch in wonder.

There's no doubt that nothing creates demand like a line of customers waiting outside your store. A line not only tells potential customers that something inside is worth waiting for, but it also sends a message of urgency. If you want *this* cannoli, you better get in line now because if you don't, they'll all be gone. That's the message the line at Mike's Pastry sends. The line creates the perception of scarcity. It is a powerful formula for brands to remember: if a brand is in demand and people believe it's in short supply, the value of the brand increases exponentially. If Mike's Pastry had twenty locations around metro Boston, the line on Hanover Street wouldn't be nearly as long because the product wouldn't be perceived as scarce. As it stands, you can only get a cannoli from Mike's Pastry at their single location at 300 Hanover Street.

Create demand. Create the perception (or reality) that your product or service is rare. Watch value increase.

In 2006 and 2007, finding a Wii console around Christmastime was nearly impossible. When stores were rumored to be getting a shipment, the line would form days in advance. People were literally camping outside electronic stores waiting for the chance to buy a Nintendo Wii! Even into 2008, two years after they debuted, the Wiis were selling as fast as retailers could order them. The Wii has become the bestselling video game system of its generation, having shipped more than 70 million consoles worldwide. While buying one today is as easy as walking into a neighborhood electronics store, in the first two years after launching, it seemed impossible to find one. Despite producing 1.8 million units each month, demand consistently outstripped supply all over the world.

Could Nintendo have physically made more Wii consoles? Of course they physically *could* have, but it wouldn't have made financial sense despite the fact that they would have sold more units and made more money in the short term. By always keeping supply lower than demand, Nintendo created urgency and excitement over the Wii. That urgency was a key factor in allowing Nintendo to wait three years before finally lowering the retail price of a Wii console. Three years is an eternity in computers and gaming! If you have a product in high demand and short supply, you can command a much higher price.

This simple but powerful formula can be best illustrated by comparing two legendary classic rock acts: The Who and Led Zeppelin. The Who came along first. Led Zeppelin followed only a few years later. Each brought their own brand of passionate and powerful British rock to the world.

In the 1970s, Led Zeppelin single-handedly raised the

art of heavy metal into the public consciousness. They were, arguably, the biggest act of the 1970s, touring the world on board their customized Boeing 720 nicknamed *The Starship*. They ushered in the decade with the awe-inspiring *Zeppelin IV* album, filled with classics like "Black Dog," "Going to California," and the ultimate rock anthem, "Stairway to Heaven."

The Who, meanwhile, rocked in the decade with their biggest album, *Who's Next,* an album that gave us two incredible classics, "Baba O'Riley" and "Won't Get Fooled Again." In 1976 they elevated their legend by turning up the volume to 126 decibels at the Valley Stadium in Charlton, London. The Guinness Book of World Records was there to acknowledge the feat and declare The Who as the loudest rock 'n' roll band on earth, displacing the previous record holder, Deep Purple, who cranked out 117 decibels four years earlier.

Both The Who and Led Zeppelin were famous for having drummers who played a larger-than-life role in the band. In most bands, the drummers were relatively anonymous, hidden at the back of the stage behind their drum kit. Many bands could lose their drummer, quickly replace him, and move on without a hiccup in their popularity. That wasn't the case with The Who and Led Zeppelin. In fact, the case could be made that these two bands gave us two of the greatest drummers in rock 'n' roll history.

Keith Moon of The Who was as innovative as any drummer of the day. He was dramatic, flamboyant, and exuberant onstage. His technique was so fluid and fast that it seemed impossible one man could accomplish so much

Keith Moon of The Who was more than just a drummer.

with only four limbs. While other drummers would play along with the rhythm section like they were supposed to, Moon would alternate between keeping the rhythm and playing along with the screams of lead singer Roger Daltry. Offstage, Moon was legendary for his excesses. He was notorious for getting drunk and trashing hotel rooms, often throwing the television set out the window before leaving the room. The most telling example of Moon's penchant for partying was a 1967 adventure at the Holiday Inn in Flint, Michigan, where Moon celebrated his twenty-first birthday after a concert. He is alleged to have stuffed the toilet full of dynamite, exploded it, and jumped out the bathroom window to avoid shards of flying porcelain. Outside, Moon apparently got inside a Cadillac, or possibly a Lincoln Continental depending on what version of the story you hear, and drove it into the hotel pool.

Led Zeppelin drummer John "Bonzo" Bonham's story is

remarkably similar. He created a drumming style based on a deep and powerful groove, and he was famous not only for the speed at which he could play but also for his hard-hitting style and the strength of his hands and feet. Bonham struck his Ludwigs with the longest and thickest drumsticks available and that sound defined many of the biggest Led Zeppelin classics. Many in the music industry consider Bonham to be the best drummer who ever played. Bonham's offstage exploits were not nearly as legendary as those of Moon, but they ended up being equally destructive.

Zeppelin drummer John Bonham was the band's heartbeat.

Moon died in 1978 when he was trying to kick his alcohol and drug habits. He was prescribed Clomethiazole, a medication he was told to take whenever he felt the craving for alcohol. On the night of September 6, after having dinner with Paul and Linda McCartney, Moon felt that dreadful urge. He impulsively took the pills one after another. He died that night in his sleep. Police determined that he had thirty-two pills in his system. Only six pills were needed to induce death.

Led Zeppelin lost Bonham two years later, nearly to the day. Bonham had been drinking heavily on the day he died, beginning with four quadruple vodkas for breakfast before rehearsals. He continued that pace until the evening, when the band retired for the night at the nearby home of guitarist Jimmy Page. Bonham fell asleep and never awoke. An autopsy revealed that Bonham had consumed forty shots of vodka in the twenty-four hours before his death and that he had asphyxiated on his own vomit while he slept.

That's where the paths of The Who and Led Zeppelin diverge. One brand went on to be revered as rock 'n' roll gold and the other became much less valuable than it should be. After Bonham's death, Led Zeppelin immediately called it quits. They released a short statement telling the world that they could not continue without their "dear friend." In their touching press release in December 1980, they said, "We wish it to be known that the loss of our dear friend and the deep sense of undivided harmony felt by ourselves and our manager have led us to decide that we could not continue as we were." By breaking up when Bonham died, the band showed a tremendous level of respect to their fans and their brand. They recognized that they were a team, and the team wasn't going to be the same without Bonham.

They have only played together for two public shows since then. In 1985, in the name of a worthy cause, they reunited for Live Aid with Phil Collins on drums. After agreeing that their performance wasn't up to standards, they refused to let any of the footage be used in the future album and video release of the event. Their next public performance was in December 2007 at The O2 Arena in London, a concert that was the most highly anticipated rock 'n' roll concert in history, with more than one million people registering for the lottery system that awarded the nearly 20,000 tickets.

That's it.

On the other hand, The Who kept going full steam ahead after Moon died. No doubt they also missed their dear friend, but they replaced him right away. They recorded two more albums before deciding to break up. In 1982 they embarked on a highly publicized farewell tour that ended in December at Toronto's Maple Leaf Gardens. Like Led Zeppelin, they reunited for Live Aid in 1985. The cause was noble enough. Then they got back together in 1988 for a 25th anniversary "Kids Are Alright" Tour. That became the "new" farewell tour.

Then, in 1996, they hit the road again playing songs from *Quadrophenia*. They had so much fun that the following summer they went out on a full-fledged tour across the United Kingdom and North America. Guitarist Pete Townshend announced at that time that he wanted to keep the band active. And active they were. They toured the world as a five-piece band in 1999 and were planning another world tour in 2002. But before they could embark on that tour, bass player John Entwistle was found dead at the Hard Rock Hotel in Las Vegas. If Moon's death didn't stop The Who, Entwistle's passing wasn't going to either. They found a new bass player and hit the road for their planned 2002 tour despite having only 50 percent of their original line-up intact. They went back on tour through most of 2006 and 2007 to support a new album, their first since 1982.

On one hand, you have to give The Who credit for surviving the death of two members and continuing on through adversity. It takes dedication to the music to soldier on through the death of the entire rhythm section of the band. Despite the challenges, The Who continued to sound great and entertain fans. They even played the halftime show at the 2010 Super Bowl. But by continuing to go on tour and record new material, The Who has pushed the supply and demand equation out of their favor. When they go out on tour, there isn't a mad rush to see them anymore. Tickets no longer instantly sell out. After all, chances are good they'll go back on tour again next year. And if you are a hardcore fan, is The Who really The Who without Keith Moon and John Entwistle?

Led Zeppelin has brilliantly created scarcity. Supply of Led Zeppelin concerts is far below the huge demand. Their 2007 reunion show was the most talked about and anticipated concert in history, and fans around the world rushed to pick up tickets knowing it might be the only chance they would ever get to see Led Zeppelin in concert. When fresh rumors of a Led Zeppelin tour started running wild again after the 2007 reunion concert, lead singer Robert Plant put them to rest by stating, "The whole idea of being on a cavalcade of merciless repetition is not what it's all about. However, it wouldn't be such a bad idea to play together from time to time."

A wise statement that clearly said that they would never be going back on a full-fledged tour, but that they might—

if you're lucky—give you the chance to see them play live now and then. So if they do plan another concert, get your tickets. Buy the concert DVD. Don't miss it. It might never happen again. Demand for Led Zeppelin in concert is very high because Led Zeppelin concerts are rare and that scarcity increases their brand value. Demand for The Who concerts is also pretty high, but demand pales when compared to demand for a Led Zeppelin show. The Who concerts are, relatively speaking, quite common. The Who is a widely available brand, easy to get.

Which brand do you want to be?

A Rock Star Five-Step Program: Famous Supply and Demand Stories

1. **Nintendo Wii.** As noted earlier in chapter six, demand for the Nintendo Wii outstripped supply by a wide margin. From the beginning, Nintendo either underestimated demand or intentionally kept supplies low. Regardless, the result was endless lines at stores that stocked the console and extremely high prices for units being offered for sale on eBay and elsewhere.

2. **Tickle Me Elmo.** The Christmas fad in 1996 was a plush toy based on the Sesame Street character Elmo Although it was less than $30 in stores, people paid as much as $1,500 a piece because supply couldn't keep up with demand. The lack of available Elmos resulted in fights between adults on a mission to get one for their child at Christmas.

3. **Cabbage Patch Kids.** More than a decade before Tickle Me Elmo, the Christmas rush was for Cabbage Patch Kids dolls. They were rolled out nationally in October 1983, and within a month, riots were happening in stores as people clamored for the limited supply. The dolls made the covers of *Newsweek* and *Time*.

4. **The Who's Cincinnati incident.** During a concert on December 3, 1979, thousands of The Who fans rushed to claim the limited number of seats nearest the stage. The result was eleven deaths and twenty-six injuries. The incident forced concert venues and promoters to rethink festival seating when seats are not assigned in advance.

continued on following page

5. **Apple launches.** For almost all recent Apple product launches, demand has far exceeded supply. Early adopters of the iPhone and iPad faced long lines to be first to own these hot products because of limited supplies. Apple fans often camped outside stores overnight to snag the limited stock that arrived in the morning.

▼

CHAPTER SEVEN

WALK THIS WAY: GETTING TO KNOW YOUR BRAND

There are two versions of the famous song "Walk This Way" by Aerosmith.

A friend of mine who's about ten years older than me loves the original. He doesn't mind the remake, but in his world the original always wins. I, on the other hand, enjoy the remake more than the original. Because of my age I heard the remake before the original, so I have a different perspective.

When Aerosmith teamed with Run-DMC for a remake of "Walk This Way" in 1986, I was sixteen years old. I was instantly hooked on the song and the two bands that performed it. The song had Aerosmith's rock 'n' roll swagger and the hip-hop street cred of Run-DMC. The remake was my entry point that led me to discover the original that was recorded ten years before. I also discovered Aerosmith's "Dream On," "Back in the Saddle," "Sweet Emotion," and hundreds of other great rock 'n' roll songs from that era. Hearing "Walk This Way" by Aerosmith and Run-DMC nudged me to explore Aerosmith further and led me to enjoy one of rock 'n' roll's greatest bands.

The following year when Aerosmith returned with the album *Permanent Vacation*, I was ready to crank up "Dude (Looks Like a Lady)" and "Rag Doll." There is no question that Aerosmith gained a whole generation of fans who grew up in the 1980s thanks in large part to their remake of "Walk This Way." The important place that remake holds in music history cannot be understated, especially when you consider where both Aerosmith and rap music were in 1986. At that time, hip-hop and rap music were in a niche far from the mainstream. Hip-hop was an American genre, with little international exposure, that was seldom heard outside of major cities. The wave of hip-hop artists that came along in the mid-1980s changed music forever and "Walk This Way" was a watershed moment.

Run-DMC was encouraged by producer Rick Rubin to record the old Aerosmith song, although they weren't initially that receptive to the idea. They went ahead with it though, inviting Aerosmith's Steven Tyler and Joe Perry to take part. The result was a song that peaked higher on the charts than the original, reaching number four on the Hot 100 chart. It also became the first hip-hop hit in the United Kingdom, peaking at number eight. Run-DMC became instant international stars and other hip-hop acts started to gain exposure. Meanwhile, other rock bands started incorporating elements of hip-hop into their music. "Walk This Way" influenced both rock and hip-hop music for many years to come.

Working with Aerosmith brought Run-DMC and hip-hop music to an entirely new audience.

The song didn't just elevate hip-hop, it also reestablished Aerosmith as a viable band. They had pretty much disintegrated in the late 1970s amid drug and alcohol abuse. They began their comeback in 1985 with the album *Done with Mirrors* but it was not successful. Despite touring heavily to support the album, Aerosmith's attempt at a comeback was not looking good until Perry and Tyler appeared in the video for "Walk This Way" with Run-DMC. The video featured Perry and Tyler in one room rehearsing and

Run-DMC in the other. After interrupting each other's rehearsals, they break down the walls between them and rock out together. For much of 1986, the video for "Walk This Way" was impossible to escape. A year later, millions of newfound Aerosmith fans were waiting when the new album *Permanent Vacation* came out and quickly went on to sell more than five million copies.

The cool thing about "Walk This Way" is that neither Aerosmith nor Run-DMC compromised their integrity or lost any fans in the process. Original Aerosmith fans may have been slightly put off by the infusion of rap music into their classic favorite, but the duet still served as a primer for the Aerosmith comeback that went into high gear in 1987. The song essentially resurrected a career that most people thought was over.

Meanwhile, fans of Run-DMC couldn't object to the homage paid to the originators of the song. In the hip-hop world, using samples from classic rock and pop songs was common. Many in the hip-hop field credit the song, and the *Raising Hell* album it was on, with spawning the "golden age of hip hop" that would heavily dominate music for the ensuing decade.

"Walk This Way" was the perfect entry point to introduce a sixteen-year-old to the Aerosmith brand and to introduce a generation of suburban teens to the new hip-hop sound. That phenomenon continues to this day with each new Rock Band or Guitar Hero game release. A new generation is hearing The Beatles, The Rolling Stones, and even Aerosmith for the first time as they play along on their Xboxes.

Your brand has plenty of existing customers who love your stuff. You need to continually serve those fans without compromise. You can't live without them. But what about all those people who *could* love you, if only given the chance to get to know you. You can advertise to them. There's nothing wrong with that strategy, except that changing people's perceptions about brands is an expensive and often painfully slow process. Sometimes it is downright impossible.

What can you do to create new entry points for customers who don't already love you? What can you highlight about your brand to appeal to potential customers without compromising your brand and alienating your core customers? Are there partnerships you can forge that would bring your brand to a new set of customers, much like Aerosmith did with Run-DMC? The next entry point you create for new customers to sample your brand could be the dawn of your brand's golden age. Or, as with Aerosmith, it might be exactly what a brand in trouble needs in order to rejuvenate.

So which version of "Walk This Way" is the better one? Apparently the remake, according to *Rolling Stone* magazine. They ranked the version with Run-DMC as 287th on their list of the 500 Greatest Songs of All Time, while the original came in at number 336.

A Rock Star Five-Step Program: A Great Brand "Entry Point"

1. **It's fresh.** Great entry points work because they offer something that people haven't already seen over and over again. If a customer isn't a fan of your brand, is it because they haven't seen your advertising? Or is it because they've seen it, and they've decided (for whatever reason) that your brand isn't for them? But when you show them something they haven't seen before, you have a fresh chance to surprise and engage them. Think of Old Spice, a brand that gained legions of new customers through their humorous "I'm on a horse" advertisements—commercials that showed potential customers something they had never seen before.

2. **It retains your core values.** Entry points only work when they connect with your brand's core values. It makes no sense to attempt to attract new customers by changing what you stand for. Both Aerosmith and Run-DMC remained true to their bands' core values in the case of "Walk This Way." Disney Cruise Line, created in 1995, provided a new entry point for the Disney brand. Until then, a Disney vacation meant packing up the family and heading to one of their theme parks in California or Florida. Disney Cruise Lines gave customers the same family friendly Disney vacation on a cruise ship traveling on the Caribbean Sea.

3. **It brings in unusual partners with similar brand values.** Ford teamed up with Harley-Davidson in 2000 to create a customized version of their popular F-150 truck. By adding a motorcycle partner to a truck, Ford and Harley definitely turned some heads. This wasn't a normal partnership,

since commonsense would suggest that Ford and Harley-Davidson are competitors, both attempting to entice vehicle buyers to choose their product. But Ford and Harley-Davidson shrewdly realized that they share common customers who have common values. By putting a Harley-Davidson logo on the F-150 truck, Ford gained a rugged, anti-establishment aura.

4. **It is temporary.** Had Aerosmith and Run-DMC followed "Walk This Way" with a remake of "Sweet Emotion" and then "Dream On," the magic would have been lost. The interesting and enticing entry point would have become pedestrian. Ford hasn't slapped a Harley-Davidson sticker on every vehicle it makes because it would no longer be special if they did. Entry points are memorable because they are often unique moments that customers remember for years to come, like the first time I heard "Walk This Way."

5. **It is genuine.** Much like the need to retain core values, brand entry points need to be genuine to be successful. If your entry point is not authentic, it will come across as a money grab. Social media outlets like Facebook have provided plenty of potential entry points for brands over the past few years, but many have missed the mark by not being genuine. Social media is a conversation, and marketers are not accustomed to dialogue. They are natural-born sellers. A brand that uses social media as a sales tool is like a guest at a party who only talks about him or herself. Brands like that are annoying. On the other hand, brands with a genuine message that goes beyond selling have a much greater chance of connecting with potential customers.

▼

CHAPTER EIGHT

THE OPPOSITE OF LOVE

The opposite of love isn't hate. The opposite of love is simply not caring. The opposite of love, when it comes to building a strong and powerful brand, is indifference.

This idea was played out one day when I was driving with my two sons. A song came on the radio, and before I even knew what it was, both of my teenage boys screamed at me to change the station. The song was by teen sensation Justin Bieber. I pried a little bit into what disgusted my kids so much about Bieber, and they provided me with a quick focus group that left nothing to the imagination. They told me how they hate his syrupy music, his squeaky voice, his look, and how all the teenage girls go crazy over him. They knew exactly what they hated about Justin Bieber. They knew his life story. There was no ambiguity.

Yet Justin Bieber draws fanatical crowds everywhere he goes. He ignites full-on riots. In an era when it's becoming increasingly impossible for a new artist to make significant money in the music industry, Bieber makes millions with his music, merchandise, and movie.

Music history is filled with Justin Biebers. Every generation has its own. Take your pick based on your age: New Kids on the Block, Backstreet Boys, Britney Spears, Bay City Rollers, Donny Osmond. Each of these acts created hysteria in their day, with millions of passionate fans and millions of others who could not stomach a note of their music.

It doesn't just apply to teen acts. You won't have to look far to find people who hate Bob Dylan, yet he's managed to carve out legendary status for himself in rock 'n' roll. He's firmly entrenched in the Rock and Roll Hall of Fame and is the only rock star to have won a Pulitzer Prize for his contribution to American literature.

How is it possible to be so despised, yet so successful?

As a rock star and as a brand, you obviously want to have fans who love you. You absolutely need them in order to be successful. If you have no fans, you have no career. You are like a business with no customers. It is as simple as that. What isn't so obvious is that whenever you have fans who love you, you will inevitably have others who hate you. It is a law of the branding universe. There's no way around it, and there's absolutely nothing wrong with it.

Take in any stand-up comedy show. You'll see someone laughing until their face hurts, and you'll find someone else whose face never breaks into smile. Read movie reviews. It is easy to find well-known movie critics who disagree entirely on the merits of a movie. One will rate it a "must-see" while another will tell you not to waste your money or time going to see it. The movie producer who needs to be worried isn't the one who made the movie that got mixed reviews. The producer who needs to panic is the one who made the movie that didn't get reviewed at all. Indifference kills movies, just like it kills brands.

Love and hate aren't really opposites in the branding world. They go hand in hand. There cannot be one without the other. For a brand, the opposite of love isn't hate. It is *indifference*.

My kids aren't indifferent to Justin Bieber. They know exactly who he his, the details of his story, and they immediately recognize his music. They can tell you numerous and precise reasons why they hate him. They are very, very specific. Could they say those things about a singer they didn't care about? Absolutely not. Bieber is well-branded. His fans know about him and why they love him, and his detractors know about him and why they hate him. What is difficult is finding someone who has no opinion about him.

Any brand that stirs up attention is bound to have detractors. It's perfect if you are getting a lot of positive feedback about your brand and then someone tells you how much they hate it. If they hate you because of what you stand for, you've done your job. They are aware of your brand and what it stands for. They understand your brand. As long as you have a greater number of people who love you, you'll be fine. On the other hand, if the world expresses a general indifference about your brand, you're dead. If people don't care, you haven't inspired passion or emotion on any level. You are ignored.

Red Bull is the number one energy drink in the world, yet it is subject to plenty of hatred and controversy. It even became the world's leading energy drink despite being banned in France, Norway, and Denmark. There are plenty of people who speak out against Red Bull, and the people who think Red Bull should be banned are clear about why. They cite health risks from heart conditions to headaches. They are very, very convincing. What is more difficult is tracking down people who don't know what Red Bull is and don't care if it is sold in their neighborhood or not. Red Bull is a rock star brand.

The New York Yankees are a rock star brand. They have won more championships than any other professional sports franchise. You see their merchandise everywhere. Millions of people love them. Yet hatred of the Yankees is, according to *Chicago Tribune* columnist Mike Royko, "as American as pizza pie, unwed mothers, and cheating on your income tax." Boston Red Sox fans would say even worse things about the Yanks. The New York Yankees are a brand that people either love or hate. There's no in-between. Good luck finding a single baseball fan who doesn't know of the Yankees and have an opinion as to whether they "suck" or not.

Rock star brands accept that having fans means having people who hate you, for whatever reason. Rock star brands fight against indifference. They stand for something, and know that they will polarize some people. Love them or hate them, rock star brands are impossible to ignore.

A BRILLIANT, BLOODY, MONEY MACHINE: HOW UFC LOVES TO BE HATED

The website Brandmojo.org, built by McGill University brand researcher Robert Mackalski, attempts to measure how people feel about various brands. The site allows visitors to express how they feel about a brand on a scale of one to five, with one being "hate" and five being "love."

At the top of the love list are some familiar and expected brands: Google, YouTube, Wikipedia, DreamWorks, and Lego, respectively. Other high-scoring brands include BMW, Disney, Haagen-Dazs, Victoria's Secret, Apple, and Coca-Cola.

On the other end of the spectrum are the most hated brands, and many of them are the likely suspects. Out of nearly 700 brands surveyed, BP ranked 663rd, proving that when you dump millions of barrels of oil into the Gulf of Mexico, your brand ranking is almost sure to sink. The major cigarette companies like Marlboro, Lucky Strike, Winston, and Camel ranked near the bottom. Not surprising, since producing a product that perpetually kills people doesn't endear you to many. But also near the cellar is one of the fastest-growing spectator sports in North America, Ultimate Fighting Championship (UFC). UFC is incredibly popular, drawing millions of fans on pay-per-view and in person to its mixed martial arts fights around the world. The UFC brand has extended from the cage to DVDs, a wealth of merchandise, video games, and action figures, all adding millions to the bottom line. Yet it hardly beats disgraced brands like Enron and BP when it comes to brands people hate.

It isn't just the general public that has a negative perception of the UFC brand. The elimination of no-holds-barred fighting was a target of Senator John McCain in 1996, when he sent a letter to all fifty governors asking them to ban ultimate fighting. The British Medical Association has campaigned to have all mixed martial arts competitions banned, as has the Canadian Medical Association. Ultimate Fighting has been banned outright in many areas, including New York, Pennsylvania, and Tennessee.

Yet despite the negative perception of their brand and the very strong public opposition to their very presence, UFC is a brand that is worth more than a billion dollars today. According to a 2009 article in *Forbes,* the brand controls 90 percent of the lucrative mixed martial arts industry. They draw, on average, more than three million viewers to each pay-per-view event and the vast majority of them are eighteen- to forty-nine-year-old men. Those are similar numbers to big college TV football games, except UFC fans are paying to watch the event. UFC draws in mainstream advertisers, including Harley-Davidson and Bud Light, who want to reach these young and influential consumers. According to Harley-Davidson Chief Marketing Officer Mark-Hans Richer, what makes UFC attractive is their "deep and passionate fan base."

What is ironic and difficult for many brands to accept is

that a deep and passionate fan base doesn't come from mass appeal. A deep and passionate fan base comes from appealing on a very powerful and emotional level to a relatively small group of people. How small? Well, if a typical match draws 15,000 fans to the venue and another three million watch on pay-per-view, the total number of fans watching a UFC bout is still less than 1 percent of the US population. If we estimate that only one in ten UFC fans pays to watch the fight on pay-per-view, it means that there are about thirty-one million UFC fans in the United States. Certainly that is impressive, but it still represents only 10 percent of the population.

The brilliance in the UFC brand is that they've embraced the idea of having 90 percent of the population dislike them. They know that to be a massive runaway success, they only need to have a positive reputation among fans of intense hand-to-hand cage fighting. And in order to have a positive reputation among fans of that style of fighting, they happily accept that the other 90 percent of the population will absolutely abhor them. If they don't accept that fact, and start to change their product to suit the other 90 percent, they will surely lose that deep and passionate fan base that makes them so much money. Watering down their intense product to please more people would *decrease* the depth and passion of their appeal, making people more indifferent to their brand.

UFC is a perfect example of how, in branding as in life itself, the opposite of love *isn't* hate, the opposite of love is indifference.

A Rock Star Five-Step Program:
Music We Love(d) to Hate

1. **Boy Bands.** Didn't anyone with any money to spend hate the boy-band phenomenon of the late 1990s? The Backstreet Boys proved that wrong with their 1999 album *Millennium*, which has sold 40 million units worldwide. That makes it equal to Fleetwood Mac's *Rumours* and ranks it ahead of Led Zeppelin's *Zeppelin IV*.

2. **Disco.** Everyone hated disco or so it seemed. But that logic is busted by the sales figures. The 1977 sound track to *Saturday Night Fever* has sold 40 million copies. Add that to the 30 million copies sold of the Bee Gees' 1979 *Spirits Having Flown*, and it appears that disco wasn't quite as universally hated as we thought it was.

3. **The Divas.** People are pretty quick to slam the screaming divas like Celine Dion, Mariah Carey, and Whitney Houston, but all that hate comes with a lot of love. Dion's 1996 album *Falling Into You* managed to sell 32 million copies. Carey did the same with her 1993 album *Music Box*. Houston topped them all with the sound track to *The Bodyguard* in 1992, selling 44 million copies. That makes it the fourth bestselling album of all time. But try finding someone who will admit to owning a copy.

4. **Billy Ray Cyrus.** Even as his hit song "Achy Breaky Heart" was climbing the charts in 1992, it seemed impossible to get anyone to admit to liking it. That makes it hard to explain the 20 million copies his album *Some Gave All* sold. It also makes it hard to explain his current celebrity status, although daughter Miley Cyrus is probably to blame for that.

5. **Spice Girls.** Say what you will, but the British girl group moved 43 million copies of their two late-1990s albums, *Spice* and *Spiceworld*. It is hard to believe that they could sell that many albums exclusively to preteen girls.

CHAPTER NINE

▼

SMELLS LIKE SOMETHING FAMILIAR

Where were you when you first heard Nirvana's "Smells Like Teen Spirit"?

If you're under forty, chances are you remember that moment. I was a young radio DJ working the night shift on an AM Top 40 station. Music on AM radio, let alone Top 40 music, was dying quickly but our station was still surviving and pumpin' out the hits. It was a Friday night, or more precisely, early Saturday morning. The program director had chosen the songs I was supposed to play. And like most late-night DJs, I knew damn well he was asleep for most of my shift, and I could probably get away with anything. I still tried to keep to the playlist as much as possible—at least until three or four o'clock in the morning when sometimes

I needed to drift off the list and play something exciting just to keep myself awake and interested.

This was one of those nights when I was dangerously close to falling asleep and letting white noise take over the airwaves. The playlist was coming in handy that night because I simply didn't have the mental energy to choose what to play on my own. The next song was just another song on the playlist. It was by a band I hadn't heard before called Nirvana. In no way was I prepared for what happened when I pushed "play" on that CD. The moment that opening riff ripped through the fuzzy late-night AM static, I was keenly aware that I was hearing something truly different. I had the pleasure of sharing it with thousands (or at least dozens) of listeners.

Almost twenty years later, the impact of Nirvana's arrival cannot be understated. It was a song, album, and band that established angst as a reasonable emotion. It gave a musical voice to a generation that had been searching for one and not finding it in the hair-band arena rock of the day, which was pretty much all about girls, booze, and cars. Nobody was speaking to a generation growing up in the shadows of the boomers, raised in the "me" decade, raised wondering what would be left of the world when our selfish predecessors were done with it. Nirvana—and the movement they were part of—sang about the realities of their generation. They were angry, confused, uncertain, proud, and ready to talk about it.

But if the music Nirvana made was *that* groundbreaking, how did it hit mainstream culture so quickly? Nirvana broke through by delivering something unexpected within an expected framework. The band gave us a sound that surprised and shocked us, yet they did it with familiar chords and harmonies that we had heard somewhere before.

"We got attention because our songs have hooks, which stick in people's minds," said Kurt Cobain when asked about the band's success. He aimed to write songs about "conflicts in relationships, [and] emotional things with other human beings."

The day that *Nevermind* reached number one, *Billboard* magazine stated that "Nirvana is that rare band that has everything: critical acclaim, industry respect, pop radio appeal, and a rock-solid college/alternative base." MTV called their music "equal parts Black Sabbath and Cheap Trick."

Songs about relationships? Pop radio appeal? Critical acclaim? Cheap Trick comparisons? Hardly sounds like hardcore alternative music.

Certainly the songs on *Nevermind* were unlike any other songs on the radio in 1991, but they were jammed with simple pop music hooks. Songs like "Come As You Are" and "Smells Like Teen Spirit" are riddled with memorable hooks that make the songs extremely accessible and catchy. Stripped down to an acoustic guitar or piano, you can hear just how melodic and hook-filled these songs really are. In music terminology, "hooks" are those attention-getting and memorable guitar riffs or lyric lines, and Nirvana songs—despite their alternative label—are laden with them. Cobain realized early on that he was doing something nobody else was doing. He was keenly aware that he was intentionally mixing two kinds of familiar sounds that hadn't really been mixed before. "It wasn't cool to play pop music as a punk band," he said. "And I wanted to mix the two."

Nirvana played *pop* music like a *punk* band. We had all heard pop music, loaded with hooks that stuck in your brain for days. And we had all heard punk bands, angry and loud and far from hook-filled. But most of us had never, ever heard pop music played by a punk band. That was part of the musical brilliance of Nirvana. They melded conflicting sounds, and brought them together to create something altogether new, yet somehow familiar. When the brain hears Nirvana for the first time, it's shocked by the bizarre combination of two known elements. Thanks to that shock, you pay attention.

Like Reese's Peanut Butter Cups! Everyone has tasted peanut butter, and everyone has tasted chocolate. But when Reese's Peanut Butter Cups combined the two as one, our brains and taste buds were forced to reconcile them into an entirely new product. Conflicting ideas awake the brain and force us to pay attention, creating a "purple cow," as Seth Godin would say. We've all seen purple things and we've all seen cows, so we can ignore them both if seen separately. But show me a purple cow, and I'm going to pay attention and likely tell everyone I know about what I've seen. Nirvana's "purple cow" was their combination of pop and punk, and we all paid attention.

Putting unfamiliar ideas in a familiar context makes the unfamiliar easier to digest. By putting raw punk music in a pop music context, millions of people were able to absorb this new sound. When introducing a new concept, consider putting it into a framework that your customers can relate to. Taco Bell says "think outside the bun," establishing that they are the fast-food place that doesn't serve burgers. For years, 7-Up marketed themselves as the "un-cola," clearly putting the unfamiliar idea of a clear drink in the familiar soda framework.

It's the same way Hollywood writers pitch movies to the studios. *Aliens* was pitched as *Jaws* on a spaceship. *Speed* was pitched as *Die Hard* on a bus. Putting the unfamiliar in a familiar context gives your brand, product, or story an immediate open door that enables new customers to join the club and become fans.

A SLICE OF SMART BRANDING: QUAGMIRE GOLF

Putting the unexpected into a familiar context has been one of the pillars to the early success of upstart golf apparel company Quagmire Golf.

There is no sport quite as steeped in tradition as golf. Where exactly golf began is a matter of debate. Eastern Scotland gets the credit for the game we know today as golf, but there's no doubt that similar stick-and-ball games were played in other parts of the world long before the first greens were manicured in Scotland. Some say golf came from the Romans; others argue it has history in Persia and the Netherlands. In recent years, Chinese researchers have presented evidence that a game very similar to golf was played there five hundred years before the modern day eighteen-hole version was introduced in places like St. Andrews, Scotland. St. Andrews is home to The Royal & Ancient Golf Club. Near the clubhouse, on the famous "Old Course," golfers have been launching golf balls down the fairway since 1552. Any sport that goes back to the rule of Mary Queen of Scots and has a home that includes the words "royal" and "ancient" in its name must be steeped in history and tradition.

With so much history, introducing change to the game and its traditions is a challenge. Even something as simple as fashion can be difficult to change. Golf has developed a stigma based on the traditional clothes that golfers have worn. For the past thirty years in particular, golfers have worn the same conservative clothing that seems designed to hide a golfer's spare tire and lack of muscle tone. Golf was never a flashy game, but at least in the Arnold Palmer glory days of the 1960s, golfers wore snug and colorful clothes. For some reason, golf fashions seemed to revert to more baggy and boring styles during the 1980s and 1990s. Fashions have hardly moved an inch in recent years, even though the game has attracted rowdier and higher-profile male and female players.

Geoff Tait and Bobby Pasternak were like a lot of young golfers growing up around the game. They loved golf, but hated the clothes. Working his summer job at the local golf course, Tait dreaded having to go anywhere after work without going home to change first. "It was embarrassing to wear the dorky golf clothing that I had to wear to work at the club," Tait said. "No chance was I picking up any chicks in that gear!" Tait and Pasternak would ditch their golf clothes and jump into trendy brands like Billabong and Hurley before they would be seen in public. Knowing there had to be many others just like them, they came to the conclusion that someone needed to create a new line of clothes for golfers, the kind of clothing that could be worn proudly off the course and on. The result was their young brand, Quagmire Golf, which makes clothes that golfers can wear on the course, having a few beers in the clubhouse, and spending the evening on the town.

Quagmire Golf did the same thing Kurt Cobain and Nirvana did with music. Cobain took traditional pop music melodies and hooks and melded them with introspective and deeply dark and personal lyrics. The result was grunge music. Tait and Pasternak started out with the style and comfort of surf and skate clothes and melded them with the tradition of golf. Their slogan, "Not fit for the fairway," says it all. Quagmire Golf has framed a new idea within a familiar context. Because of that context, people are instantly able to grasp what Quagmire Golf is all about. It doesn't take a lot of explanation or drawings or graphs. Golf clothing in surf and skate style—a new idea that makes immediate sense to everyone.

Having a concept that was easy to grasp was vital for Quagmire Golf, especially in the early days when nobody knew who they were and wouldn't take their sales calls. The boys would meet with buyers and golf pros and run head-on into golf's tradition. "The older guys were stuck in their ways of buying these traditional shirts and pants from the same companies that they had for years, and the styling and colors were much the same every year," Tait said. "When we came onto the scene it was a bit of a shock to their systems."

Since the concept was easy to explain, Tait and Pasternak were able to persuade a few open-minded buyers at prestigious private golf clubs to give Quagmire Golf clothing a shot in their pro shops. When two well-known southern Ontario clubs, the St. Thomas Golf Club and the Hamilton Golf Club, both started carrying Quagmire's line, the rest of the industry took notice.

Today, every aspect of the brand instantly tells the story of golf clothes with style. All advertising, catalogs, and web content portrays the brand's vibe and attitude. Even when Quagmire Golf considers sponsoring a professional golfer on a tour, they make sure that golfer embodies the brand. They look for the right attitude, looks, and body structure to make sure the brand's essence is never lost for even a moment. That includes Chez Reavie, who scored his first win on the PGA tour at the 2008 RBC Canadian Open while wearing Quagmire's clothes. Today, PGA tour members Aron Price and Matt Weibring proudly wear Quagmire Golf's clothes.

The latest evolution for Quagmire Golf is Color Fusion: shirts that change color with the heat. The next time you see a tense playoff hole at a PGA tournament, you might just see one golfer's shirt change color under the sun and the extreme pressure of sudden-death playoff golf. If you do, thank Tait and Pasternak at Quagmire Golf for merging two concepts into something new and exciting for golf, just like Nirvana did for music twenty years earlier.

A Rock Star Five-Step Program: The Other Seattle Bands

Nirvana gets all the credit, but the early 1990s grunge movement out of Seattle wasn't a singular effort. There were several other important Seattle bands that helped to change the face of music.

1. **Pearl Jam.** There seemed to be a Nirvana/Pearl Jam rivalry in the early grunge days, but that has long since disappeared. Pearl Jam's longevity and versatility has firmly established their place in rock history.

2. **Alice in Chains.** Probably the darkest of the Seattle bands, they were set back by the 2002 death of lead singer Layne Staley from a drug overdose.

3. **Soundgarden.** Chris Cornell and the band channeled classic rock as much as they waved the grunge flag.

4. **Foo Fighters.** Dave Grohl played drums in Nirvana, but he stepped to the front of Foo Fighters. Like Nirvana, Foo songs are rich in catchy hooks. Unlike Nirvana, life in the Foo Fighters seems much happier.

5. **Temple of the Dog.** Members of Soundgarden and Pearl Jam came together to honor Andrew Wood, a friend who had died of a heroin overdose. Wood was the leader of several influential bands in the area. The 1991 *Temple of the Dog* album only became legendary years later, when Soundgarden and Pearl Jam emerged as rock stars.

CHAPTER TEN

DEATH BY HYPE: LEARNING FROM AXL'S MISTAKES

Remember the dud that was *Chinese Democracy* by Guns N' Roses? Listening to it now, years removed from its wildly overhyped release, it really isn't such a bad album. It is actually a pretty damn strong collection of songs.

In hindsight, the critics were pretty kind to *Chinese Democracy*. Although today most people look back at the album as a colossal flop, *Entertainment Weekly* gave it a B- rating and *Rolling Stone* gave it four stars out of five. Those who took the time to get to know the album seemed to enjoy it. So why is *Chinese Democracy* destined to be remembered as a failure? Simple. It didn't live up to the hype. Realistically, it never even had a chance. The quality of music hardly mattered. *Chinese Democracy* would have had to sell millions upon millions of copies for it to have been successful when it was released. And it would've had to sell as many copies as the legendary *Appetite for Destruction* for it to have been seen as worth the wait, money, and anticipation.

It simply couldn't have been good enough to match the advance billing as the most expensive recording project ever made. It could never live up to the expectations of fans who waited eighteen years between new Guns N' Roses' albums. Over the course of those years, there were many leaks, sneak previews, and boastful comments by Axl Rose and others. The album was called "fucking epic" and "mind blowing" by Skid Row singer Sebastian Bach. At least once a year there was some talk of this incredible but mysterious project that Axl Rose was working on. Periodically, songs would leak out on the Internet. Radio stations would get them on the air and rush to play them as much as possible before the record company served them with cease and desist orders. This dance went on for years.

For nearly two decades, we heard about this incredible album. From early on, it had the *Chinese Democracy* name attached to it. It had people talking. Release dates were set and then pushed back. The bar kept getting raised higher and higher. What did that do for expectations? Most smart marketers could have predicted the fate of *Chinese Democracy* without ever hearing a note of music.

The same problem greeted Sammy Hagar's band Chick-enfoot, a so-called "super group" featuring Hagar, Van Halen bassist Michael Anthony, guitar wizard Joe Satriani, and Red Hot Chili Peppers drummer Chad Smith. Sammy Hagar's marketing plan for Chickenfoot's 2007 debut album was driven purely by hype, as if Axl Rose were advising him on his promotional strategy. Although Chickenfoot didn't take eighteen years and $13 million to make their album, Hagar spent plenty of time talking tough about how groundbreaking their debut album would be.

Axl Rose spent nearly two decades and over $13 million making *Chinese Democracy.*

"When people hear the music, it's Led Zeppelin," Hagar bragged. "I know that's a bold statement, but it's as good as that. It's ten times Van Halen."

As good as Led Zeppelin? Ten times Van Halen?

Those are two of rock music's most revered bands. Does

it really make sense to raise expectations that high? Doesn't it set you up for failure to suggest that your work will eclipse the very best?

Chickenfoot's debut album wasn't exactly *Zeppelin IV* or Van Halen's epic *1984* in music or in sales. There was no "Stairway to Heaven" or "Jump" to leave a lasting impression upon the world. The debut album by Chickenfoot has never appeared on any best-of lists. It's never been suggested, by anyone other than Hagar himself, that Chickenfoot was comparable to Led Zeppelin and ten times better than Van Halen.

Rock star brands understand that communicating with a sense of humility and honesty will win over more fans than empty, boastful hype. Rock star brands know how to under-promise and over-deliver. Sounds simple enough. You want to entice people and tease them with your soon-to-be-released product, but you don't want to hype the product to the point where the eventual release is a letdown.

The prequel to the initial *Star Wars* trilogy suffered from the same problem. George Lucas made us wait two decades. We endured endless advance hype, making it almost impossible to truly appreciate the newer *Star Wars* movies in their own right. The movies became instant must-sees, and nearly as quickly became an easy target for those letdown by Jar Jar Binks, soporific dialogue, and marginal storylines.

Remember the advance hype on the Segway? For years we heard rumors about a new project under the guidance of inventor Dean Kamen. Speculation about exactly what Kamen was working on was everywhere. We were told this mysterious invention would change the way cities were built and the way human beings interacted. The invention, under the code name Project Ginger, was billed as possibly being bigger than the Internet and as important as the invention of the personal computer. Kamen helped fuel the fire by telling people his invention would "sweep over the world and change lives, cities, and ways of thinking."

On December 3, 2001, the Segway made its debut on *Good Morning America.* It was a nifty little machine, built with amazing dynamic stabilization technology that reacted to subtle body movements. The makers boldly predicted their machine would reach $1 billion in sales faster than any product in history. When they went on sale via Amazon.com In November of 2002, sales didn't quite take off as predicted. Today, the Segway is a decade old. Did it change the way cities are built and the way human beings interact? Did it sweep over the world and change lives? Not at all, unless you're Paul Blart, mall cop, and you now have something cool to ride. There's nothing wrong with the Segway. It is an innovative vehicle, but there was never any hope that a single device could change the world the way the Segway was predicted to.

Although these days Apple products are subject to ridiculous amounts of prerelease anticipation, the company almost always finds a way to provide unexpected features that pleasantly surprise their fans and live up to expectations. Almost always. But in 1993 Apple miscalculated and put a tremendous amount of advance billing behind a new device that they claimed would revolutionize how people and businesses managed their time and their lives. The device was called a personal digital assistant, or PDA. The official name was the

Apple Newton. Between development, promotion, and marketing, Apple is rumored to have spent more than $1 billion on the Newton.

CEO John Sculley started the hype-machine rolling at the 1992 Consumer Electronics Show in Las Vegas when he demonstrated it publicly for the first time. The problem was that the product was nowhere near ready. As the hype increased, so did pressure on Apple developers to rush the Newton to market. Apple was forced to get the product on store shelves before it was truly perfected, resulting in a machine that was too slow, too large, difficult to use, and far too expensive at $1,000. With sales expectations that were as high as the anticipation itself, Apple was disappointed when Newton sold only 100,000 units in its first year.

The Newton only lasted a few years before being shelved. Still, a few legacies persist from the Newton days. First, the name "PDA" didn't exist until it was applied to Newton. Second, the essential idea of a tablet-like device like Newton didn't die. While it is widely regarded as an expensive failure, there is no doubt that Newton served as a seed from which grew the iPod, iPhone, and iPad.

There is a fine line between building anticipation for your product and hyping your product to the point of dooming it. The right amount of honest anticipation helps make for a successful product. Too much hype and you are destined to let your customers down. In fact, it could be argued that hype itself is negative. The word implies a method of exaggerating things, overstating them, and artificially creating interest in something. "Hype" is often used to describe a questionable dealing, scam, or deception. Hype is a negative; "honest anticipation" is its natural positive. Hype often leads to disappointment, regret, and low sales. Honest anticipation often leads to surprise, delight, and profits.

For *Chinese Democracy* and Chickenfoot, like Segway and Newton, it was game over, before it even began.

HOW BAD WAS *CHINESE DEMOCRACY?*

This book isn't about rating albums; it is about the wonderful connection between great bands and great brands, and what makes them so successful. The *Chinese Democracy* project makes for an interesting study because if you take the critics' word for it, the album should have been a success. Yet it wasn't, for reasons other than music. The reasons that it is viewed as a failure go far beyond music and into the realm of brand identity, marketing, and perceptions.

So what did critics think about *Chinese Democracy*? The answer is surprising, considering the negative vibe around the album. Metacritic.com, a website that aggregates reviews of music and movies, gave *Chinese Democracy* a Metascore of 64 out of 100. The album, according to Metacritic, garnered "generally favorable reviews." Here is what some of the higher-profile rock critics had to say about it:

▸ "The first Guns N' Roses album of new, original songs since the first Bush administration is a great, audacious, unhinged, and uncompromising hard rock record." —*Rolling Stone*

▶ "A ton of musical food for thought here, requiring several listens before the nuances are revealed."
—*Billboard*

▶ "It's an exhilarating album. Seriously, after finally hearing these fourteen tracks in their finished form I was so energized I wanted to climb a mountain."
—*Boston Globe*

▶ "It's actually pretty damn good. It rocks, often pretty hard." —*No Ripcord*

▶ "It's touching on a human level. Noble even. I didn't think he had it in him."
—Robert Christgau of MSN Consumer Guides

A Rock Star Five-Step Program: Lessons on Anticipation from Apple's Steve Jobs

Today Apple is more careful than they were in the Newton days. The Newton was developed under CEO John Sculley, the man who forced out founder Steve Jobs in 1985. Jobs returned in 1996 after the Newton fiasco and has since guided Apple to incredible success. There are three valuable lessons about building anticipation that we can learn from Jobs:

1. **His lips are sealed.** Apple always keeps new gadgets just secret enough to delight and amaze people with their release. A good example is the release of the iPhone 4G in 2010, which was something only rumored to exist until a mysterious phone was found in a California bar. This unusual, never-before-seen phone had the look and feel of an Apple product as well as distinctive Apple logos, but matched nothing on the existing Apple roster of products. The "misplaced" phone made it into the hands of tech weblog *Gizmodo*, where it became one of the most discussed topics on the Internet. Was this a prototype of the iPhone 4G? Apple refused to comment, and eventually they worked through the courts to retrieve their misplaced phone. A few months later it made its debut to incredible sales. Some believe the "lost" iPhone was planted, put there so that hype could be amassed for the newest generation of Apple's iPhone. Plant or not, that phone left behind at a bar by an Apple employee did exactly that. It created plenty of press and excitement, months before the actual product debuted.

continued on following page

2. **He sees it like a customer.** Jobs and Apple always try to take a customer-driven approach to new products. When they create something new, they examine all of the angles from the user's point of view. When they created the iPod, they didn't just create a music storage and playback device. They created a music store, iTunes, to go with it. That was an essential step because there needed to be an easy way for users to find and install music for the new device. While solving that problem, Apple created what turned out to be the largest music store on earth and an incredible profit machine for the company! It is vital for all companies to look at their products from the customer's perspective, asking, "Could a person actually use this product?" and "What problem does this product actually solve?"

3. **Jobs takes it personally.** Advance excitement for Apple products is driven in large part by the personal passion that Jobs exudes. He is a natural salesman, masterful at transferring confidence to everyone in the room. His personal confidence soon becomes yours. He speaks from the heart and mind, seldom referring to notes and written statements. He talks about the personal investment that his team has made in the product and focuses on how it will benefit people in their day-to-day lives. Watching Steve Jobs unveil a new Apple product, it may appear that his comments are unprepared and unscripted, but there is no question that each speech takes tremendous preparation. Jobs is not alone in preparing product releases. Each one is constructed like a movie so that they appear to be fluid and natural. Jobs knows that his personal role

in building anticipation for Apple products is vital to their success. His personal touch is a key part in establishing honest anticipation instead of empty hype.

4. **Show us, don't just tell us.** When Steve Jobs reveals a new product, he doesn't just hold it up. He uses it. He makes it work and shows you exactly how it functions, in front of millions of eyes. Jobs doesn't hype something that might be coming, like Axl Rose did. Instead he stands before you, device in hand, and shows you just how remarkable it really is.

5. **"And one more thing."** It is a famous line in Apple circles. At nearly every product launch, just when you think you've seen it all, Steve Jobs comes up with "one more thing" to show you. It feels like he has so much to share with you that he simply can't remember everything at once! Walt Disney called them "weenies," those little extras that draw you in. Disney felt the spire on top of Space Mountain; Cinderella's castle; and the many gates, bridges, and trails leading to each attraction were all extras that help to build anticipation. Steve Jobs uses "and one more thing" as an Apple weenie. It is another unexpected extra that draws you in and makes you want whatever he is selling even more!

CHAPTER ELEVEN

YOU GOTTA SERVE SOMEBODY

Bob Dylan doesn't care about you or what you think or what you want from him. I realized that very quickly the first time I saw him live. It seemed like that night Dylan was in a mood to play his fast songs slow and his slow songs fast. If it was originally an acoustic song, Dylan played it plugged-in and vice versa. Dylan played the music the way *he* wanted to that night, the same way he has been playing for more than forty years. Dylan has spent four decades making music that matters to him, speaks to the causes he feels strongly about, and tells the stories he wants to tell.

In his early days, he captured the mood and spirit of a generation with songs like "Blowin' in the Wind," "The Times They Are A-Changin'," and "A Hard Rain's Gonna Fall." That type of music wasn't dominating the charts at the time, but it was the music that Dylan wanted to make. Very soon people were talking about America's new folk-music poet. When the world had become aware of Dylan the folk singer, he plugged in and shocked the 1965 Newport Folk Festival with an electric set. Because he wanted to. He was booed on stage at Newport that day, but he played on and played loud.

Dylan followed Newport with the release of a six-minute epic song called "Like a Rolling Stone." Six-minute songs aren't exactly made-for-radio hits, but Dylan wasn't making his music for radio stations. Dylan made "Like a Rolling Stone" for himself. It turned out that many of us felt the same way Dylan did about that song, which *Rolling Stone* magazine later called the greatest song of all time. Bob Dylan's career went in and out of favor over the next three decades as he recorded electric rock, folk music, country songs, sound tracks, roots music, collaborative albums, gospel music, and a Christmas album. The latter two albums were even more unusual given Dylan's upbringing in the Jewish faith.

Every step of the way, Bob Dylan was always uniquely Bob Dylan. Dylan's path was not one that any before him or after him have taken. There is no logic that suggests anyone could have done what Dylan has done. As J. Hoberman wrote in *The Village Voice,* "No iron law of history demanded that a would-be Elvis from Hibbing, Minnesota, would swerve through the Greenwich Village folk revival to become the world's first and greatest rock 'n' roll beatnik bard and then—having achieved fame and adoration beyond reckoning—vanish into a folk tradition of his own making."

"A folk tradition of his own making" is a great phrase to describe Dylan's path. Dylan's choices were seldom guided by what was popular at the time, what others were doing, or what trends seemed to be emerging. Dylan's career was guided by his passion.

Bob Dylan has always been driven to sing about topics he is passionate about, regardless of commercial appeal.

Great brands are driven by that same type of passion and meaning that Dylan is known for. For grocery store chain Whole Foods, that passion is its mission to change the way the world eats. It isn't profit or shareholder value that defines the decision-making process at Whole Foods. CEO John

Mackey believes those things will come about as a result of passionately pursuing their mission. That mission has created a completely different type of shopping experience.

Whole Foods, growing rapidly from their initial start in Austin, Texas, has brought to Main Street, America, a new level of awareness around organic foods and sustainable farming. That core mission, to change the way the world eats, dictates what type of food they stock and sell, where and how they purchase their food, how their stores are designed and powered, and how they treat their customers. The US Environmental Protection Agency has lauded the chain for its use of alternative power sources. In a 2006 Harris Interactive/*Wall Street Journal* poll, Whole Foods had the best "social responsibility" score of any company on their list of America's best and worst corporate reputations. Whole Foods has also helped establish nonprofit foundations to protect marine life and to educate farmers on animal compassion. They were among the first to eliminate nonrecyclable plastic bags from circulation, and they have a company policy of donating 5 percent of their profits to charitable causes.

Do those things directly increase profits? Obviously not. But they do play a vital role in changing the way the world eats and that mission has fueled the growth and profit margins of Whole Foods over the past decade. They commit to these things because their entire brand is built around them and being true to that brand is what makes them profitable. Customers choose to shop at Whole Foods, certainly not the least expensive grocery store, because of what the company passionately stands for. To not do these things would mean an instant and dramatic reduction in customers and the loss of the meaningful vision that defines the brand.

Like Bob Dylan's music, the Whole Foods mission isn't necessarily driven by popular opinion. It is driven by a passionate belief in something and a desire to share it with the world.

Clothing retailer Lululemon Athletica has taken the same approach in turning the world on to their line of upscale, yoga-based fashions. The very first store, opened in Vancouver in 1998, was inspired by founder Chip Wilson's belief that yoga was the optimal way to maintain strength in athletics. Only thirteen years after that first store opened, Lululemon is a $500 million publicly traded company, and they continue to offer free, in-store yoga classes. They have continued to maintain their focus on the promotion of yoga as a means to better health and a happier life. You don't have to shop at Lululemon to take a yoga class with them. They encourage people to take the classes regardless of how much money they spend in the store or what type of clothing they wear when they show up. Lululemon's mission begins with yoga, and the profits—and there are plenty of them—flow from there.

A Rock Star Five-Step Program: Branding Like Bob Dylan

1. **Sing anthems, not songs.** Anthems are songs that, figuratively speaking, make you stand up, remove your hat, and pay attention. Songs are fun, but disposable. Anthems last forever. There's nothing wrong with songs. Songs are easy to sing along to, enjoy in the moment, and reminisce about years later. But they don't make long-term impressions. Songs are popular for a few months, but they're quickly replaced by a new crop of songs.

   Anthems, on the other hand, can change you. They have the power to alter opinions and influence people. They might not be as popular in the moment as sing-along songs, but they remain popular for long periods of time. Anthems are nearly impossible to duplicate and they are not easily replaced. "The Times They Are A-Changin'" is certainly an anthem. So are "Blowin' in the Wind," "Hurricane," "Like a Rolling Stone," and "Tangled Up in Blue." Dylan writes and sings anthems.

   In branding, this is the difference between a company that makes a low-cost alternative product and a powerful brand name, such as a generic soda and Coca-Cola. A company that makes generic brand soda is simply singing songs, enjoyable for those who consume them in the moment, but easily replaced by other generic brand sodas. Consumers making soda purchasing decisions based on price are quickly lured away by the cheapest available option. Nobody develops loyalty for the low-cost generic brand. Consumers that make their soda purchasing decisions based on taste are not easily lured away by a cheaper option because they are purchasing a product they perceive to taste better. That's where Coke—the anthem—always wins.

2. **Forget about the money.** Okay, this isn't an easy one. At least *try* to forget about the money. If you are focused on profit, you are focused on you, not your customer. Focus on your customer, and profit will come, as Whole Foods has learned by focusing on changing the way the world eats. Dylan never made music explicitly for profit. Even when he was a rising performer on the folk scene at age twenty, Dylan said "I just want to keep on singing and writing songs like I am doing now. I just want to get along. I don't think about making a million dollars. If I had a lot of money, what would I do?" Dylan didn't sit down to write rock 'n' roll's greatest song when he wrote "Like a Rolling Stone." He just wrote a Bob Dylan song. It connected with people, and because of that connection, the song went on to become a classic.

While Ben & Jerry's ice cream is certainly a profitable company, many of their projects and actions are not driven by profit, but instead by social conscience and their hippie-like attitude. In September 2009, they renamed their ice cream flavor "Chubby Hubby" to "Hubby Hubby" in support of gay marriage. The tub featured a drawing of two men getting married under a rainbow—a perfect publicity move driven by passionate beliefs and attitudes, not solely by profits. Ben & Jerry's knows that by following their mission, profit will flow. When you stop trying to make money and please the

continued on following page

masses, you give yourself the chance to create art that will truly make you rich.

3. **Embrace social change.** Like any good folk songwriter, Dylan has a keen sense for recognizing and tapping into social movements. People tend to associate Dylan with protest songs, but Dylan has written very few songs that are about specific social causes and movements. Dylan's songs have been regularly adopted by various movements, such as campaigns for racial equality or the anti-Vietnam War movement, yet Dylan never appeared to be writing about the cause-of-the-moment to cash in on what was hot. Dylan benefited from being associated with all of these societal movements because he outwardly embraced change.

4. **Create your own mountain.** Becoming a rock star brand is going to be tough, but it is going to be nearly impossible if you set out to conquer someone else's mountain. If your plan is to launch a new brand of toothpaste to take on Crest, you are in for a long battle with Procter & Gamble. The toothpaste mountain is pretty crowded and will be defended by some formidable fortifications. On the other hand, if your plan is to create an entirely new kind of tooth-care solution, you might find yourself as the king of your own mountain. It is always better to create an entirely new product category, or variation on an existing product category, instead of attempting to conquer an existing product category.

Bob Dylan didn't set out to try and become the next Elvis Presley. That mountain was taken. Instead,

he became the only and the very best Bob Dylan, and
nobody has knocked him off that mountain yet.

5. **Sing from the heart.** Dylan has always recorded songs from
   his heart or songs written by others that spoke to his
   heart. It takes great courage to put yourself on the line
   like that, but that's what great artists do. Putting your
   personal feelings, fears, and opinions out in public is
   dangerous because inevitably someone will dislike your
   feelings, fears, and opinions. While they might alienate
   some people, they will be strongly embraced by many
   others. These are your fans. Forget about everybody else.

CHAPTER TWELVE

HONESTY: YOU CAN'T FAKE IT

Billy Joel's schmaltzy ballad "Honesty" spoke the truth back in 1979. Yet at the time, the accepted strategy for building a brand was creating perceptions that were often far removed from reality. Honesty was not a widely accepted strategy for marketing before the digital revolution that hit us in the late 1990s. Today, growing legions of brands are discovering that honesty is essential in developing a loyal fan base. They are learning the lesson evident in rock 'n' roll for years: exposing your faults and imperfections makes you more real, more human, and more likely to be loved.

The Beach Boys recorded a song in 1965 that demonstrates how authenticity is a timeless value. It is a song that I've always loved, but I was never quite sure why until I began to analyze the bond between brands and their fans. This particular song oozes authenticity. The Beach Boys had been in the studio that day for hours and hours recording and desperately needed a break. As fun as being in a band is, spending endless hours doing take after take of the same song is fatiguing and can really suck the life out of what should be a fun process.

During that stressful recording session, some friends of the band came by the studio, including Dean Torrence of Jan & Dean. Mike Love went across the street to buy a few cases of beer. With each take, and each subsequent beer, the recording session began to gradually morph into a party. The songs got crazier and crazier. People started to improvise and mess around. Drummer Hal Blaine pounded on anything within his reach, including an ash tray at one point. Everyone in the room joined in the singing, even if they didn't know the words. Brian Wilson, with Dean Torrence helping him out, kept raising his voice above the incessant talking and laughing around him, until he could resist no more and gave in to the laughter himself.

Thank God that the tapes never stopped rolling because the final product became a number two hit in December 1965. "Barbara Ann" remains one of the Beach Boys most endearing songs, forty-five years after the studio party ended. One of the reasons people still love this song so much after all these years is the brilliant honesty that it exudes. The Beach Boys were not the only band leaving some of their mistakes in the final mix. The Beatles songs like "Taxman" and "The Long and Winding Road" are only two of many to feature stray guitar notes, drumming mistakes, and various unusual microphone noises. The Beatles were famous for their mistakes, outtakes, and experiments. Producer George Martin was wise to leave many of them in because they made the songs more interesting, intriguing, and human.

Rumor has it that the famous repeated eight piano notes that open "Old Time Rock 'n' Roll" by Bob Seger were a mistake. The recording equipment accidentally played it back twice, and Seger and his producer loved the way it worked and left it in.

The song that features what *Guitar World* magazine called the number two guitar solo in rock history was itself a mistake that was never supposed to exist. Eddie Van Halen was warming up for a gig at the Whisky A Go-Go in Los Angeles and started tapping out scales and improvising in the studio with a piece the band had been playing live for a few years. Producer Ted Templeman was rolling tape. In Van Halen's words, "It was just a total freak thing. It was just an accident. He happened to be rolling tape." The result was a gem called "Eruption." On the album *Van Halen*, it is the track right before "You Really Got Me." To this day true fans cannot hear "You Really Got Me" without hearing "Eruption" first. They have melded it into one classic piece of rock 'n' roll. Not only was "Eruption" itself never supposed to exist, but the final mix even includes a mistake. "I didn't even play it right," Van Halen told *Guitar World*. "There's a mistake at the top end of it. Whenever I hear it, I always think 'Man, I could have played it better.'"

Even in the days of four-track analog recording, George

Martin, Brian Wilson, Bob Seger, and Eddie Van Halen all had the ability to create audio perfection. They didn't need to leave mistakes in. Yet they intentionally did over and over again because the imperfections enhanced the song.

There was a point, only a few years ago, where having a solid rock star brand meant covering up every wart and imperfection. When something went wrong, companies rushed to cover things up and often issued a "no comment." Before the rise of the Internet and social media, companies could cover up blemishes with image advertising. They could bury their skeletons and paint a perfect picture for their customers. In those days, it was all about money. You could buy your way into any image you wanted to create and very little could be done to get in your way.

Today the power base has shifted, and now the customer has equal, or even greater, power. Treat your customer poorly and instantly hundreds of people know about it through Facebook and Twitter updates. Provide bad service at a hotel or restaurant and instant reviews on Travelocity and other sites will have an immediate impact. If you make a mistake today, there is no way to hide from the discussion. Many brands still choose to ignore the discussion, but the discussion happens nevertheless. Because of this never-before-seen level of connectedness, today's brands need to be more authentic. There is no longer any way to buy enough advertising to combat persistently negative word-of-mouth campaigns because social media allows word-of-mouth to reach more people faster than any advertising possibly can. Smart brands today engage their customers in two-way dialogue. Using social media, brands can acknowledge their flaws and mistakes when things go wrong, and they can share with their customers the steps they are taking to improve. Cable giant Comcast is a great example of a brand that has tried to dramatically reverse poor customer satisfaction scores through social media. In 2008 they started to actively use Twitter to monitor customer problems and intervene to solve them proactively. Their once-dismal customer service scores have improved each year.

Some smart brands have even decided to make their imperfections a part of their appeal. What if you had a product that was repulsive to use, but worked brilliantly? The old-school approach would be to ignore the bad taste and use your marketing budget to promote the effectiveness. The old-school approach would be to spend enough money telling people your version of the story so that they would ignore the reality. Canadian cough medicine Buckley's did not take that approach. Their cough medicine doesn't taste very good. In fact, it tastes awful. But it has a track record of working very well. Buckley's could have spent their advertising budget telling people how well the product worked and attempting to mask the reality that it tasted horrible. They wisely decided to turn this weakness into a strength. Why fight the obvious? Buckley's slogan is, "It tastes awful, but it works."

Brilliant. The advertising message begins with a concept that everyone who has ever used the product can agree on—

it tastes awful. Making the message even more powerful is the widely held notion that medicine *should* taste awful. After all, a medicine that tastes like candy can't possibly be as effective as a medicine that tastes awful. That's the way the human mind thinks about medicine! Entire generations were raised on medicine that tasted awful. By basing their advertising message on reality and honesty, Buckley's has become incredibly successful. Their TV campaigns are fantastic, and their Internet videos are wildly popular. Buckley's has built a brand based on authenticity and honesty.

Marmite is another product that, to most palates, tastes awful. True, it is loved by many in the United Kingdom, Australia, and New Zealand. But to the vast majority of the world, Marmite tastes horrible. Like Buckley's, the makers of Marmite decided not to fight the obvious. They chose to embrace it, flaunt it, and revel in it. Visit them at Marmite.com and instantly you'll be presented with two options to click on. One says "I'm a lover" and the other reads "I'm a hater." You get a different version of the website based on your choice. It takes a brave (and smart) brand to allow people to publicly declare their hatred for its product on the front page of its website!

If you choose "I'm a hater," you can take part in the campaign to "stop the spread." You can add to the list of "ten ways to ruin a sandwich," all of which use Marmite. The site even includes a suggested recipe using roadkill to mask the taste of Marmite! Of course, the "I'm a lover" version of the website is much kinder to the controversial product. But both versions of the website facilitate discussion about the brand, and the very fact that they outwardly acknowledge that many people hate their product is grounds for discussion.

A point to consider about honesty in branding: We human beings are wonderfully imperfect creatures, and we can only relate and bond with other wonderfully imperfect creatures. We can't possibly form a bond with something that has no flaws because flawlessness simply doesn't exist. If you are attempting to create a bond between a human being and a product or a giant faceless corporation, you are going to have a tough time. On the other hand, creating a bond between a human being and an imperfect, living, breathing brand is much easier.

HONESTY IN BRANDING: THE TYLENOL STORY

One of the most stunning examples of how powerful honesty in branding can be is from the fall of 1982, when seven people were killed by poisoned Tylenol capsules. Remember, in 1982 there was no social media. There was no Internet. In 1982, a brand could still easily issue a "no comment" and buy its way around almost any negative publicity.

However, this was different. The deaths ignited a nationwide scare, with hospitals receiving hundreds of calls every day from people who were terrified after taking Tylenol. This was far too big to ignore. The makers of Tylenol,

Johnson & Johnson, made a decision to go on the offensive in handling the crisis. They immediately mounted a campaign that stands up today as one of the best in public relations.

First, they didn't try to deny the relationship between the deaths and their product. That would have been the first step for many companies, but Johnson & Johnson never did that. Instead, Johnson & Johnson pulled every Tylenol product from every store shelf and hospital in America, despite the fact that the deaths were confined to Chicago's West Side and only to those who took Tylenol's Extra-Strength caplets. The company didn't need to recall all thirty-one million bottles of Tylenol product everywhere in the country, but they did it despite the immense cost. Consumers who had purchased caplets were offered free replacements at a cost of millions of dollars to Johnson & Johnson. They did this despite the fact that there was likely not a drop of cyanide poison in any of the caplets exchanged.

Instead of hiding from the disaster, the company immediately suspended all advertising for Tylenol, and publicly joined forces with the Chicago police, FBI, and Food and Drug Administration to help find the source of the problem. As the search for the culprit went on, Johnson & Johnson offered a $100,000 reward for solving the mystery. They also took the lead within the industry to quickly develop new tamper-proof packaging. Johnson & Johnson's actions were about as transparent as any company's had ever been in handling a crisis, and they were met with widespread praise for how they reacted.

When the crisis was over and it was time to rebuild the brand, Johnson & Johnson continued to be open and transparent. They held a press conference to demonstrate their effective new tamper-proof packaging. They embarked on a massive advertising campaign, punctuated by discount coupons. Sales representatives scheduled presentations to medical professionals all over the country to show the steps that Johnson & Johnson had taken to restore confidence in the product. The steps Johnson & Johnson took gained them tremendous positive media coverage in major newspapers and national magazines. The Tylenol comeback became a news story unto itself. And what a comeback it was!

Before the crisis, Tylenol held a 37 percent share in the lucrative over-the-counter analgesic market. That was the summer of 1982. Immediately after the disaster hit, their share plummeted to just 8 percent. By December 1982, Tylenol had already climbed back to 24 percent of the market. In the ensuing years, Tylenol reclaimed its market position and to this day remains a dominant pain-relief medication.

The story is remarkable, but even more so when put in an historical perspective. The reaction of Johnson & Johnson appears more like the reaction of a cutting-edge tech company with a socially aware public relations department schooled on the wildfire spread of information on the Internet. But this was 1982 and none of those things existed. There was no school of thought that taught companies how to deal with a crisis this big. So what guided Johnson & Johnson as they navigated these turbulent waters? Their executive team was guided by a credo written in 1943 by their founding father, Robert Wood Johnson, that reads:

> *We believe our first responsibility is to the doctors, nurses, and patients, to mothers and fathers, and all others who use our products and services. In meeting their needs, everything we do must be of high quality.*
>
> *We must constantly strive to reduce our costs in order to maintain reasonable prices. Customers' orders must be serviced promptly and accurately. Our suppliers and distributors must have an opportunity to make a fair profit.*
>
> *We are responsible to our employees, the men and women who work with us throughout the world. Everyone must be considered as an individual. We must respect their dignity and recognize their merit. They must have a sense of security in their jobs.*
>
> *Compensation must be fair and adequate, and working conditions clean, orderly, and safe. We must be mindful of ways to help our employees fulfill their family responsibilities.*
>
> *Employees must feel free to make suggestions and complaints. There must be equal opportunity for employment, development, and advancement for those qualified.*
>
> *We must provide competent management, and their actions must be just and ethical.*
>
> *We are responsible to the communities in which we live and work and to the world community as well. We must be good citizens—support good*

*works and charities and bear our fair share of taxes.
We must encourage civic improvements and better
health and education.*

*We must maintain in good order the property we
are privileged to use, protecting the environment and
natural resources.*

*Our final responsibility is to our stockholders.
Business must make a sound profit. We must
experiment with new ideas. Research must be carried
on, innovative programs developed, and mistakes
paid for.*

*New equipment must be purchased, new facilities
provided, and new products launched. Reserves must
be created to provide for adverse times. When we
operate according to these principles, the stockholders
should realize a fair return.*

That simple credo, almost seventy years old, remains a
guiding light for the company to this day, and you can easily
access it on their corporate website. Although it was written
decades ago, it is entirely valid in today's hyper-information,
social-media age.

A Rock Star Five-Step Program: Avoiding the Two Deadly Words

We live in an age where "no comment" no longer works. Today those are the two deadliest words you can use when you are trying to build a trustworthy brand. Sure it worked years ago when big companies could deny and deflect when things went wrong, but today our world is so interconnected that "no comment" serves no purpose other than to invite more questions and doubts.

So what do you say when the media is hounding you for a comment? How can you avoid saying anything dangerous or incriminating and still provide an honest comment? Today's smart public relations experts offer up more honest and human answers that are straightforward and plausible. Instead of "no comment," consider phrases such as:

1. "I would really like to answer your question right now, but unfortunately I cannot." Simple and direct, this is slightly better than offering no comment at all.

2. "Our first obligation is to those involved, and once we have thoroughly spoken to those people, I will be happy to answer your question." This transfers a sense of greater responsibility and can help defer questions.

3. "We are working hard to confirm all of the facts involved, and once we've done so, I will be in a position to answer your question." This makes it clear that even though you can't say much, you are not sitting by idly as the situation unfolds.

4. "There are a lot of missing pieces to this puzzle right now and our team is committed to understanding the situation thoroughly. I should be able to answer your question

when that process is complete, which should be later this afternoon." When you use a phrase like this, you are letting people know that you are actively involved in fixing the situation and you are giving them a firm expectation as to when they can expect more information from you.

5. Offer a reminder of the stakes. If jobs and careers are at stake, don't hesitate to say, "I'm sure you'll understand that while I would really like to answer that question, we have an obligation to speak first with those directly affected."

▼

CHAPTER THIRTEEN

CASHING IN ON OLD (SPICE) BRANDS

E very so often there is hidden equity discovered in a brand that appears to be dead, but with the right amount of TLC proves to be very much alive. That's what Old Spice and Johnny Cash have in common.

Old Spice was originally a women's perfume when it launched in 1937. A year later, Old Spice for men made its debut. For years the famous clipper ship logo dominated men's grooming. The brand's popularity appeared to have long since sailed by the time the men's grooming market really took off in the 1980s. By that time, Old Spice was widely viewed as the cologne your dad would wear. In the 1980s, in vogue products like Polo by Ralph Lauren had surpassed Old Spice, and the sinking trend for Old Spice continued into the 1990s, when Procter & Gamble bought the brand from the founding company, Shulton.

Was it time to kill Old Spice? Procter & Gamble didn't think so. They embarked on a plan to rebuild the faded brand, launching a series of new products geared toward a new, younger generation. Some stuck and some didn't, but the brand did eventually start to gain traction. Humorous marketing played a major role in the comeback, with actors Neil Patrick Harris (*Doogie Howser, M.D.*) and Bruce Campbell (legendary B-movie actor) appearing in commercials for Old Spice. With the explosion of social media outlets like YouTube, these commercials spread virally and gave the brand a tremendous lift with young consumers.

However, the true catalyst for restoring Old Spice as the top-selling men's grooming brand was a series of commercials that debuted during the Super Bowl on February 8, 2010. The commercials, called "The Man Your Man Could Smell Like," became Internet sensations and have garnered millions of views online in addition to millions of impressions on TV. Procter & Gamble followed the original commercial with several others in 2010, and then followed those with a three-day YouTube campaign in which the actor, Isaiah Mustafa, answered nearly one hundred questions from fans on Facebook, Twitter, YouTube, and other social media platforms while in his "Old Spice guy" character. The commercials solidified Old Spice's place as the leading men's grooming brand and created instant celebrity status for Mustafa, an aspiring actor and former professional football player.

The story of Old Spice isn't that different from the story of "the man in black." Around the time that Old Spice was giving way to Ralph Lauren, Johnny Cash had long since given way to a new generation of country singers. After his successes as an outlaw country star in the 1960s and 1970s, nobody was playing Johnny Cash on their Sony Walkman in the 1980s. Although he continued to draw fans to his concerts, his new songs were not making an impact on the charts. In his autobiography, Cash wrote that he felt he was actually "invisible" in the 1980s, and that his record label of many years, Columbia, was indifferent to him and not interested in his new music. So to get their attention, Cash intentionally recorded an awful song, a self-parody called "The Chicken in Black" about Cash's brain being transplanted with that of a chicken. Ironically, the song was actually Cash's commercial high point of the decade. Not long after the song was released, Cash parted ways with Columbia Records for good.

It appeared that the Johnny Cash brand was done. And then something special happened. A new record company, American Recordings, offered Johnny Cash the chance to record again. This new company was better known for their hard rock and hip hop artists, but producer and label owner Rick Rubin saw something in Cash that fit with his vision. Together they created the 1994 album *American Recordings*. The album was sparse, recorded in Rubin's living room and featuring only Cash and his guitar. Critics instantly hailed it as the best work Johnny Cash had done since the 1960s, and it won that year's Grammy Award for Best Contemporary Folk Album. Cash himself said that his warm reception at the 1994 Glastonbury Festival in England was a high point in his career. It was clear at that point that Cash was back.

Despite being diagnosed with a form of Parkinson's disease and diabetes, Cash recorded a series of *American Recordings* albums, each one containing personal and poignant songs selected by Cash and Rubin. His cover of the song "Hurt" by Nine Inch Nails received particularly widespread attention and acclaim, and today it is widely recognized as his epitaph. The *American Recordings* albums remain a must-have for fans of both Johnny Cash and modern music. The late Johnny Cash is permanently cool and genuinely missed. Few musical acts have made a comeback as astonishing and deserving as the one Cash mounted in the decade before his death. He went from being a forgotten-about archive from the Hall of Fame to a six-time nominee at the 2003 MTV Video Music Awards.

How were Old Spice and Johnny Cash able to mount such successful comebacks? What do these two disconnected brands share in common, and what can your brand learn from them?

First, they changed their message and started telling a new story.

Old Spice brilliantly adapted their message to the self-deprecating, tongue-in-cheek tone of today's youth. Their commercials began to spread virally on the Internet, spawning websites dedicated entirely to Old Spice commercials.

Johnny Cash changed his message too. Instead of recording country or gospel songs, he recorded songs originally performed by hard rock bands like Nine Inch Nails, Soundgarden, U2, Tom Petty, and Danzig. His *American Recordings* albums also included his own songs, but the albums kept a consistent and very personal tone.

Second, they made some new friends and partners.

Old Spice collaborated with advertising agency Wieden and Kennedy to create advertising that was edgy and in touch with young consumers. Wieden and Kennedy is best known for their work with Nike, and they've also developed many cutting-edge campaigns for Coke, ESPN, and Miller beer. They weren't the kind of agency you'd normally associate with Old Spice, and Procter & Gamble was not the kind of company that would normally use Wieden and Kennedy. This unnatural fit was a perfect recipe to deliver results that surprised people and captured attention.

Johnny Cash collaborated with Rick Rubin to create music that was edgy and in touch with young consumers. Rubin is a producer famous for starting Def Jam records and working with performers like the Beastie Boys, Run-DMC, Red Hot Chili Peppers, and Metallica. This was also a very unnatural match, and the result was once again surprising and captivating. Finally, they didn't give up. They forged ahead despite the naysayers. They knew that rebuilding a damaged or nearly forgotten brand is not a quick fix.

Old Spice began their turnaround in 1990 when it was purchased by Procter & Gamble. In 1992 they updated the logo and color scheme. Over the next fifteen years, they released a fresh line of body washes, body sprays, deodorant sticks, and shaving products. When the new Old Spice brand became popular, they rereleased the original blend with the slogan, "If your grandfather hadn't worn it, you wouldn't exist." The turnaround wasn't instantaneous, but Procter & Gamble was committed to Old Spice.

Cash began working with Rubin in 1994, and won a Grammy for Best Contemporary Folk Album for *American Recordings*. Certainly that album met with plenty of critical acclaim, but it was the subsequent volumes, particularly volume four of the series, that truly cemented Cash as a contemporary icon. Five months before his death, Cash released "Hurt," and the song became so identified with Cash that the original singer of the song, Trent Reznor, proudly stated, "That song isn't mine anymore." Johnny Cash was not an overnight success the second time around, but Rubin and Cash were committed to the project.

New messages and stories that appeal to a changed marketplace, new partners and collaborators that add credibility and enhance the story, and a never-say-die attitude can, against the odds, bring a faded brand back to life.

A Rock Star Five-Step Program: Overcoming the Perception Gap

Brands that fail to differentiate themselves are the most at risk of becoming obsolete. The huge problem is that a gap exists between what the brand *makers* and the brand *users* think. People who are making products, and are very close to them, believe their brands are well differentiated, but those who are buying brands off store shelves don't see the differences as clearly. In fact, a 2009 survey by Bain & Company noted that while 80 percent of CEOs believe their product to be unique in the market, only 8 percent of consumers agree!

The company making the toothpaste believes that its new formula clearly differentiates its product from the competition, but to the average consumer it is just another brand of toothpaste with little to differentiate it from the dozens of other brands on the shelf.

Here are some ways that brands can overcome the perception gap:

1. **Be remarkable.** If you don't create buzz, you die at the hands of competitors who do. Old Spice created buzz, as did Johnny Cash. That conversation helped to spread the word about what made them unique. Brands that generate buzz have a head start when it comes to differentiation because people are already talking about them.

2. **Consider the marketing as an integral part of the product and vice-versa.** The most compelling marketing stories are based around incredible products that create memorable customer experiences. Great stories make for gimmick-free marketing.

continued on following page

3. **Reach out on new platforms.** Smart brands today tell their story through discussion and dialogue on multiple platforms. Brands that are active in social media have a chance to not only tell their story, but demonstrate their story, one customer at a time.

4. **Use show-and-tell in your marketing.** If you are introducing a product that's different, don't just make claims in your marketing. Instead, clearly demonstrate your differences. Provide proof. Show the analytical left brain the empirical evidence it needs to believe.

5. **Continue to reinforce "different" as an essential element of your brand, even after you've established yourself.** Southwest Airlines got their foot in the door by promoting their low-cost difference. Even though they've since become the number one passenger airline in America, they continue to reinforce that same difference—low cost—at all times.

▼

CHAPTER FOURTEEN

THE POWER OF
THE INCOMPLETE

eppelin IV. One of rock's greatest albums. Nothing written on the front of it. No band name. No album name. Just a strange picture and four hand-drawn symbols. In fact, the album's official name isn't even *Zeppelin IV*, but it has been referred to that way as a consequence of the band's previous habit of numbering their albums.

Would *Zeppelin IV* have been a bigger success if they had written "Led Zeppelin" across the front? Not likely.

One of the very cool aspects of this classic album is the mystery behind the strange cover.

What does it mean?

What do the symbols mean?

Why didn't they put their name on it?

The utter lack of information on the cover became a

serious point of discussion for fans, spreading word about this very cool album.

How about *The White Album* by The Beatles? It didn't have a name either. It was just a stark white album with the words "The Beatles" discreetly embossed on the front. Like *Zeppelin IV*, this album didn't have an official name but was given the handle *The White Album* by fans.

Would it have been bigger if they had called it *A Doll's House* as originally planned? Nope. Once again, the intrigue created by the lack of any visual markings on the cover helped create a mystique around the album. The seeming lack of any design or artwork is part of the legacy of the album, and at the time was a point of intense discussion among fans. The technique that Led Zeppelin and The Beatles were using is often called "white space" or "negative space" in the advertising world. But in the case of both *Zeppelin IV* and *The White Album*, it turned out to be positive. Both albums are often cited among rock's very best. *Zeppelin IV* sold more than 32 million units worldwide, making it one of the bestselling albums in history. Meanwhile, *The White Album* ranked tenth on *Rolling Stone* magazine's list of the 500 Greatest Albums of All Time. The Beatles and Led Zeppelin were tapping into the *power of the incomplete.*

Did they do it on purpose? Did they know what they were doing?

Perhaps not, but many great artists throughout history have consciously made an effort to leave a few things out. The power of the incomplete can be traced back to Donatello, the Italian Renaissance sculptor. Many art historians credit Donatello as the first artist to understand the power of the *non-finito*. He used the concept to create ideas within his work, instead of striving for a "perfect" finished work. The incomplete nature of the piece conveys to the viewer a sense of the "poetic frenzy" that Donatello felt inspired his best work.

Fast forward a hundred years, and you can see the same influences at work in the sculptures of Michelangelo. He left sculptures partially entombed in stone and intentionally left many things looking unfinished in order to capture attention because the human eye sees a world in motion, not as a still picture. The *non-finito* provided that sense of motion and allowed the viewer to mentally complete the picture.

Around the same time, Leonardo da Vinci was incorporating the technique into his paintings. He used a different term, *sfumato* meaning "smoky," but it created the same powerful impact. Da Vinci made the lines on the face of the *Mona Lisa* intentionally smoky, blurred, and almost incomplete in order to engage the mind. Like his contemporary Michelangelo, da Vinci knew that no real human being's world is made up of static lines. By blurring the lines on her face, the *Mona Lisa* took on a lifelike quality that captivated the viewer. "Confused shapes," said Da Vinci, "arouse the mind." Today, we continue to be captivated by her. In December 2010 media outlets were buzzing with the news that researchers had found tiny numbers and letters hidden in her eyes, only visible by a magnifying glass, which only contributed to the painting's legacy.

It might be hard to believe, but a popular burger joint in the Southwest has a lot in common with those classic artists.

In-N-Out Burger doesn't call it *sfumato* or *non-finito*. They call it the secret menu. Actually, *they* don't call it that, but their customers do. In-N-Out Burger only has four food items on their menu: the hamburger, the cheeseburger, the double double, and french fries. Yet there are literally dozens of "secret" menu items you can order at every In-N-Out Burger. The menu never acknowledges them. The staff never talk about them. Yet you can walk into any In-N-Out Burger and ask for "The Flying Dutchman" or a "3 by Meat, Animal Style" and you'll get exactly what you asked for, no questions asked, even though these particular items aren't on the menu. Part of the allure of In-N-Out Burger is the secret menu. It draws interest. It intrigues the mind. It is in large part what makes their grand openings into events that attract thousands of people and news helicopters!

To further the mystery and intrigue around the brand, In-N-Out Burger discreetly prints Biblical references on the containers and wrappers of their food. Hidden under the milkshake cups you'll find the phrase "Proverbs 3:5," and on your cheeseburger wrapper you will see "Revelation 3:20." Like the hidden messages inside *Mona Lisa*'s eyes, In-N-Out Burger entices their customers with a sense of mystery.

Volkswagen tapped into the power of the incomplete in

1959 with their famous "think small" campaign. *Advertising Age* ranked this advertisement number one on its list of the top one hundred advertising campaigns in history. This ad also brought the idea of "white space" to the forefront of modern advertising. It used a tremendous amount of white space and very small text to communicate the essence of the brand. Not only did it communicate that essence, but it also got people talking and helped to sell millions of unusual little gas-friendly European cars in a North American market dominated by Detroit's large gas guzzlers. The VW Beetle changed the landscape of the American auto industry forever, and that simple ad played a vital role.

When you stay up late watching a bad movie to the very end, you are experiencing the power of the incomplete. Same thing when you watch a football game that appears out of reach at halftime. The power of the incomplete works because the human mind hates loose ends. Despite the fact that the movie sucked or the game was a blow-out, you watched right to the bitter end because the human mind would rather put up with a crappy movie or game and go to work tired than deal with the loose end of not knowing what happened! Our minds are always seeking a resolution to tie together loose ends in the world around us.

In the case of the Volkswagen Beetle ad, the white space plays an important role. It engages the mind. That much white space sends a message that the brain cannot ignore, and you are compelled to read on and find a resolution to the loose end, even if your interest in a small, gas-friendly European car is minimal.

What does your brand intentionally leave out? Would you ever "think small" like Volkswagen did?

Do your customers have a secret menu to order from?

Are there secret codes hidden in your product?

Do you have the guts to release an album without your name on it?

Creating a little mystery around your brand will go a long way toward engaging the minds of your customers.

A Rock Star Five-Step Program: Tapping the Power of the Incomplete

1. **"Animal" by Def Leppard (1987).** This song, from their album *Hysteria,* was painstakingly put together by the band and producer "Mutt" Lange over the course of two-and-a-half years. The band said it was the most difficult song on the album to get right, but it also proved to be a massive hit around the world. Near the end of the song, as the chorus repeats, the entire song comes to a startling halt. After a few seconds of silence, it kicks in again with a final refrain of the chorus

2. **"A Day in the Life" by The Beatles (1967).** This classic song uses the power of the incomplete near the end, as the band holds the final piano chord for forty seconds. It remains one of rock 'n' roll's most famous final chords. All of the members of the band played an E chord simultaneously on different pianos. In the studio, they kept increasing the recording level to capture the fading sound. As the level increased, the studio noise became audible, including a squeaking chair and rustling papers. The silence that closes "A Day in the Life" is every bit as much a part of the song as the piano notes that open it.

3. *Smile* **by The Beach Boys (1966-1967).** This album was intended to be the follow-up to the incredibly successful *Pet Sounds* album. Using the same progressive recording techniques that created the number one hit song "Good Vibrations," Brian Wilson envisioned creating a master-piece. Unfortunately, his deteriorating health, escalating drug use, and other pressures put the project on hold and the album was left unfinished. Over the course of thirty

continued on following page

years, *Smile* became the hottest album that never was, as bootleggers and collectors shared what little elements of the album were leaked. Finally, in 2004, Wilson completed the album thirty-seven years after he started it, and without the help of the original band. While Wilson's solo version was well-received, fans still clamored for the original. Early in 2011 the band finally announced that they would be releasing the album under the title *The Smile Sessions*.

4. **"The Look" by Roxette (1989).** This song used the power of the incomplete in two ways. First, it was a mystery to many when Minneapolis radio station KDWB started playing it. They had been delivered a copy by a US exchange student who bought it while in Sweden, where the band was already popular. When KDWB started playing it, there was a sudden rush in America to find a copy of "The Look" because it was a rare import until EMI Records could get a copy rushed out to hungry fans. Second, like Def Leppard's "Animal," the song comes to a complete stop near the final chorus before picking up again.

5. **"Shakin' All Over" by Chad Allan & The Expressions (1965).** When this Canadian band recorded a version of Johnny Kidd's "Shakin' All Over," they had an instant number one hit in Canada. With the British Invasion in full swing, the record company didn't want US radio stations to know that this new song was by a Canadian band. To create mystery around it, they released the song in a white label with the words "Guess Who?" on the front. It worked . . . almost too well! The song went to number two on the US charts and led Chad Allan & The Expressions to change their name to The Guess Who.

▼

CHAPTER FIFTEEN

THE SEX PISTOLS AND THE ART OF GETTING ATTENTION

I n late 2009, we lost a brand-building legend when Malcolm McLaren passed away. Those familiar with McLaren know him as the manager of the Sex Pistols and as an eclectic solo performer and artist. Although he is well known in music for his accomplishments, he is relatively unknown in business circles. And he shouldn't be. McLaren was a master of the 360-degree brand, seeing the band he managed as much more than a musical entity. McLaren was first a clothing designer, and he realized that if he could convince influential bands to wear his clothing, sales would take off. The idea of celebrity endorsements wasn't new at the time. It was how McLaren went about it that was revolutionary.

McLaren targeted the buzz band the New York Dolls to wear his clothes onstage. However, by the time he approached them with his idea in 1974, the band was dangerously close to breaking up under the weight of addictions and infighting. So instead of becoming their tailor, he became their manager. McLaren got them into rehab and kept the band together long enough to see his clothes grace the stage and watch sales take off because of it. However, the reunion didn't last. When the band broke up, McLaren returned to running his clothing store full-time. But this time he had a vision of how his sense of fashion could help create an entirely new kind of band and brand.

In 1975, McLaren met a young man with bright green hair wearing a Pink Floyd shirt on which he had written "I hate" above the band's logo. McLaren loved the kid's style and attitude, and immediately hired him to be the lead singer of a new band he was creating. He named his new protégé "Johnny Rotten," and he introduced him to the musicians he had already assembled. McLaren wasn't creating a band the traditional way, where musicians get together organically and find a certain magic. McLaren was creating a product, strategically putting together the pieces of the puzzle that would eventually become his vision of the Sex Pistols. Johnny Rotten was going to be the face of the band.

The Sex Pistols weren't simply about music. They were about an image and a lifestyle. Amazingly, the band only recorded one studio album together before breaking up. Despite that lack of material, they still managed to secure a place in the Rock 'n' Roll Hall of Fame thanks to the tremendous influence they had over pop culture by inspiring the late-1970s punk movement. In the years after their debut album, hundreds of bands emerged from the United Kingdom and the US inspired by the Pistols. Guns N' Roses, The Clash, Billy Idol, Green Day, Nirvana, and Oasis are among the many bands that trace their influences back to the band that *Rolling Stone* magazine ranked at number fifty-eight on their 2004 list of the 100 Greatest Artists of All Time.

What did McLaren understand about building a brand that many before (and after) him failed to fully understand?

McLaren knew that a great brand isn't one dimensional. "Christ, if people bought the records for the music, this thing would have died a death long ago," said McLaren in 1977. In their first review in the influential *NME* magazine, Sex Pistols guitarist Steve Jones declared, "Actually we're not into music. We're into chaos." Indeed, the Sex Pistols were equal parts about look, message, attitude, reputation, and timing as they were about music. Everything the band did and said became part of their brand identity. In the early days, the band grew their notoriety when they were banned from two influential clubs because of the fights that would inevitably break out during their performances, often involving—or at the very least fueled by—the band themselves. Rotten was developing a stage presence that involved smashing gear, throwing chairs, and even walking off stage to sit with the audience. The Sex Pistols were cutting their chops musically and building a legend at the same time. Their actions, words, look, and sound all contributed to the eventual brand. It was far more than just music.

McLaren realized that great brands market to masks, not reality; they market to people's aspirations—their masks—and not their realities. Jimmy Buffett sells office drones an escape to the Caribbean to be the beach bum they envision themselves as. Harley-Davidson sells CEOs the hardcore rebel image they crave. The Sex Pistols sold the working-class youth a revolution against the Queen, the government, and the established order of England in the late 1970s.

Unlike most people at the time, McLaren knew that PR is the new advertising. McLaren was a master of manipulating the media, making audacious statements that made for excellent quotes, and creating stunts that got wild attention. He was keenly aware that PR was critical to the band's success. Press was golden, whether it was good press or bad press. McLaren made no apologies for what he called "sleeping with the media" in the name of PR. One of the most famous PR incidents became known as the "Grundy Incident," in which the band was interviewed live and uncensored on British TV's *Today* program. Host Bill Grundy endured a two-minute disaster as guitarist Steve Jones repeatedly swore at him, calling him a "dirty bastard" and "fucking rotter" on live TV. The incident grabbed national headlines, as obscenities were extremely rare on British TV. The band's antics garnered them the front page of the *Daily Mirror,* which ran the headline "The Filth and the Fury."

McLaren knew that, in the case of the Sex Pistols, even the worst PR was actually great PR. That strategy came to a peak in 1977, during Queen Elizabeth II's Silver Jubilee celebrations. The Sex Pistols had just released a song called "God Save The Queen" with lyrics that attacked the monarchy and all that it stood for. Perfectly timed to capitalize on the Silver Jubilee, McLaren put his band on a barge and sailed them along the River Thames to play the song outside the British Houses of Parliament. The police raided the boat, arrested McLaren, and the Sex Pistols enjoyed massive press coverage. That press coverage was the catalyst for the band's success. They became the poster child for the working class of England who wanted to spit in the face of the establishment.

While most brands strive to appeal to the masses, McLaren knew that in order to be loved by everyone, you need to be hated by someone else. Superman is nothing if there is no Lex Luthor. Batman is pointless without The Joker. The Sex Pistols mattered because so many people—parents, government officials, the church, school officials, the upper crust of society—hated them. Without that hate, the band's purpose would have evaporated. London councilor Bernard Brook-Partridge was outspoken in his criticism of the band, calling them "unbelievably nauseating" and "the antithesis of humankind." Even some employees at the band's record company, EMI Music, refused to handle the band's single as it emerged from the plant.

How much do people hate you when they refuse to do their jobs because they object to being associated with you?

It didn't matter to McLaren. He wisely realized that the only way to appeal passionately to the (relatively) small group of fans he had was to piss off the vast majority. The more he could alienate the majority, the more passionate the minority would feel for his band. There could be no indifference toward the Sex Pistols. McLaren was visionary in his understanding of branding. There's a lot to be learned from McLaren and the Sex Pistols, and I'm not saying that simply because the guitarist and I share the same name.

GIVE THEM SOMETHING TO TALK ABOUT— GETTING NOTICED MCLAREN STYLE

McLaren did it over and over again with the Sex Pistols: he gave people something to talk about. He put his band on a barge in the Thames to serenade the Queen. He created unforgettable moments on live TV. His band notoriously destroyed nightclubs. If McLaren did one thing right, he created "buzz" and used PR to spread the word about his band.

We human beings long to connect with one another through stories. Give people a great story, and they'll tell it over and over again. It could be through the never-ending, twenty-four-hour news cycle, social media, or face-to-face discussion. Great brands give people something to talk about and tap into the incredible value of public relations to do their marketing for them. That applies equally to the smallest small businesses as it does to the biggest advertiser on the planet!

Marc Pritchard, the CEO of Procter & Gamble, told

Ad Age magazine that the future of marketing is inextricably linked to PR. The company found out firsthand how powerful PR could be when they launched the Old Spice "Man Your Man Could Smell Like" campaign during the 2010 Super Bowl. "PR was able to give our big ideas a megaphone that we used to spur participation that helped lead to spontaneous combustion," Pritchard said. "PR is a great amplifier, builds relationships, and invites consumer participation."

Procter & Gamble, with all of their endless financial resources, knows that if you give people something to talk about, you can light a fire and your story will be told for you. But you don't need a multibillion ad budget to do exactly what Procter & Gamble does. In fact, small local businesses often have the best opportunities to tap into the power of PR. For a small business, getting positive PR starts with a great story.

Kathy Pickus and Terri Goodwyn had a great product they believed in, but no budget to tell the world about it. They turned to PR to launch the Dot Girl First Period Kit, a kit to prepare young girls for the arrival of menstruation, an issue some parents have trouble addressing with their children. Dot Girl built a network of connections with reporters, bloggers, and writers who specialized in topics like teen health, puberty, and family issues. With a solid story to tell, they were able to secure several product reviews in newspapers and magazines. According to Pickus, each piece of PR became a tool of leverage to "convince the next reporter to write about Dot Girl products."

So far, results have been fantastic. Their PR-first strategy has landed them in *The Globe & Mail,* the *Seattle Post-Intelligencer*, and on CNN and CNBC.

It helps that Dot Girl has done their homework. They don't just tell the story of their product, but they focus instead on the story of *why* their product is important. Citing a 2010 study in *Pediatrics,* they note that puberty is arriving earlier that ever before in young girls, with breast development starting as young as age seven. The earlier onset of puberty is catching many parents off guard, leaving their daughters lacking the information they need about their bodies' changes. Dot Girl aims to bridge that knowledge gap by preparing girls for what is to come. The story in the media became the increasingly early arrival of puberty, and Dot Girl was able to piggyback their product as the solution to the problem discussed in that news story. To that end, they have also created a "What's Normal?" bookmark that is distributed free to schools and nonprofit organizations to help disseminate vital information for children and parents. Armed with that information, parents become much more likely to consider investing in a Dot Girl First Period Kit.

One of the great takeaways from the Dot Girl story is simple: if your product solves a problem, look for news stories about the problem itself. If you've done your homework like Dot Girl had, any news story about the problem is a likely opportunity to profile your product as a potential solution.

A Rock Star Five-Step Program: The Path to Positive PR

1. **Build relationships.** You should know all of the writers, bloggers, reporters, and editors who deal in your area of expertise. Develop solid two-way relationships with these people so that you are seen as a trusted ally and not someone taking advantage of an opportunity.

2. **Write articles.** Consider writing short articles about your field of expertise. Do not focus the articles on your business, but instead focus on the general problem you solve. A home builder who writes articles about innovative new home designs will probably quickly develop a reputation as someone who is knowledgeable and trustworthy. If newspapers and magazines won't accept your articles, start a blog. In fact, you should probably start a blog anyway.

3. **Speak publicly.** Hand in hand with writing about your field, offer to speak to others about it. Make yourself available at no charge to community groups who are looking for a speaker. A home security expert who speaks to a neighborhood watch group can probably count on some sales as a result.

4. **Be playful.** People want to do business with people who are passionate about what they do. You should exude fun and enthusiasm for your field. There are very few professions where having fun isn't a positive thing.

5. **Be remarkable.** Like Malcolm McLaren did with the Sex Pistols, do remarkable things consistently and publicly. A bakery that gets involved in the community by baking the biggest birthday cake in history is going to get plenty of PR. Being remarkable is the biggest key to getting PR.

▼

CHAPTER SIXTEEN

DIFFERENT BEATS
BETTER

Wicked Lester was one of the million early-1970s rock bands in New York City. In America's largest city, live music is always easy to find and it was no different in 1972 when Wicked Lester recorded their one and only album. These guys were just another rock band, better than some and worse than others. Their eclectic mix of music never really caught on, and late in 1972, the two founding members decided to put Wicked Lester to bed and form a new band to start the new year.

They came up with a new name and recruited a few new members, and in early 1973 they made their debut to an audience of three people at the Popcorn Club in Queens. By the end of the year, the band that played a concert for three people had signed a record deal, debuted their first album, and were about to hit the road for a North American tour. Within a few years, they were one of the biggest-selling acts in the world and they continue—to this day—to draw thousands of fans to every single concert they play.

What did this new band do right that Wicked Lester had done wrong? How were the same guys able to turn things around within a year and become so much more successful?

The band originally called Wicked Lester didn't become the world's greatest musicians and songwriters overnight. They couldn't possibly do that. What Wicked Lester decided to do instead was to be different. They changed their name, focused on harder-edged rock, put on elaborate make-up, and created alter-ego, comic-book inspired personalities. In 1973 Wicked Lester became the band you know today as KISS. The two men at the heart of Wicked Lester, Gene Simmons and Paul Stanley, remained the core of KISS. They didn't suddenly become the very best at their craft, but they brilliantly (and suddenly) became unique. Instead of attempting to be better, they became different.

KISS created an image unlike any other band and became one of the biggest rock acts of the 1970s.

The problem with "better" is that everyone has his or her own version of it. While on a business trip to New York last year, I was invited to dine at Per Se in the Time Warner Center. Thomas Keller, the man behind Per Se, is one of the most respected restaurateurs in the world. Per Se was ranked as the ninth best restaurant in the world by *Restaurant Magazine.* It has the highest designation possible, four stars, from the *New York Times.* Full disclosure: I didn't enjoy my meal. The service was fantastic. The food preparation and presentation was amazing. I understand why Per Se is so well-respected. Unfortunately, the meal served just didn't suit my tastes. My experience at Per Se is a perfect example of why being "better" isn't the ideal strategy: everyone has a different opinion of what constitutes excellence.

The "best" car, according to experts, will probably disappoint someone who wants a powerful and tough 4x4 capable of taking on any terrain. The "best" TV show, according to entertainment critics, regularly attracts only a small percentage of the overall population, the rest of whom choose to watch other programs. What one person thinks is best clearly isn't always best for everyone else. Being "better" is entirely subjective.

Another problem with attempting to be better is that it usually makes your brand more indistinguishable from the market leader. If you want to make a portable music player that is better than the Apple iPod, chances are good you'll end up with a portable music player that is very similar to the Apple iPod. On the other hand, if your mission is to make a portable music player that is unlike anything else in the world, you will more likely end up with a product that stands out, for better or for worse, against the competition.

Does a Rolex keep better time than a Timex? The answer is probably yes, but will the owner of a Timex be late for a meeting with the Rolex owner? Not likely. Both watches keep time just fine. They both meet the basic level of time-keeping quality that watch buyers demand. So why does one sell for less than $50 and the other start at more than $5,000? The Rolex is perceived to be of higher quality, but the reality is that the average watch buyer will never know the difference between the two watches based on timekeeping quality alone. One is a status symbol, and one is a watch. Once a basic level of quality is met between two products, the advantage goes to the brand that distinguishes itself: the brand that is unique.

Both a Porsche and a Honda will be equally reliable when it comes to getting you to work on time, day in and day out. One will cost you more than $100,000 and the other less than $20,000. Can the average car buyer determine the difference between the Porsche and the Honda based on quality alone? Hardly. But the average car buyer can easily determine the difference between the two brands based on look, feel, sound, and image. Porsche is a brand that stands out.

In the cases of Rolex and Porsche, one of the features that distinguishes each brand and makes them stand out against their competitors is price itself. There is a natural inclination for buyers to see the price tag and *assume* a certain level of quality, even if they cannot possibly determine what that might be on their own. Quality *is* important. To suggest that clearly inferior products can beat higher quality ones at the same price point is wrong. You can't create things that don't work and expect to have sustained success. But once a basic level of quality is perceived by the customer to have been met, the brand's differentiating factors become the basis for their success or failure.

A great example of how brand image transcends brand quality is water. Which brand of bottled water is better, Dasani or Aquafina? That depends on who you ask. Dasani is distributed by Coca-Cola, Aquafina by Pepsi. Both brands promote the word "pure" in their marketing. Dasani claims it is "enhanced with minerals for a pure, fresh taste." Aquafina, on the other hand, promotes that their water is stripped of all minerals to offer "Pure water, perfect taste." Both brands spend millions of marketing dollars every year to convince you that one brand of water is more refreshing, more pure, and better tasting than the other. The reality is that both brands come from the same basic source: the public water supply. Certainly both Dasani and Aquafina each have treatment processes that are unique to their brand, but the fact remains that the water you are buying from each of them is simply treated tap water.

On the ABC news program *20/20,* John Stossel and crew did an in-depth project to determine if bottled water drinkers could differentiate between the various brands. They compared Aquafina, Iceland Spring, American Fare, Poland Spring, Evian, and plain old New York City tap water. It was definitely a rather unscientific survey conducted on the streets of New York, but the results were clear. The most expensive bottled water, Evian, was the definite loser. And the cheapest brand of bottled water, K-Mart's American Fare, was rated as the best-tasting water of the bunch. New York City tap water did just fine, coming in at the middle of the pack.

But maybe it isn't taste that differentiates the bottled water brands. Maybe, as the advertising would lead you to believe, drinking bottled water provides a health benefit over drinking tap water. Not so, says *20/20*. They ran standard New York City tap water past the microbiology team at the University of New Hampshire, where they determined that there was no difference between bottled water and tap water. Run a bottle under a tap and fill it with water, and you get the same product you currently pay $5 a gallon for. If gas flowed freely from a tap, would anyone be at the gas station buying it? Of course not, so why are we all willing to pay for bottled water?

Simple. Bottled water is *different* from tap water and that difference has created an image of a healthier product. People believe it is better for you, even though it has been scientifically demonstrated over and over again that it isn't.

Wicked Lester didn't need to improve their musicianship exponentially to go from unknown bar band to world-dominating rock band. They did, however, need to differentiate themselves in a substantial way to become KISS. KISS is living proof that a brand's unique image is more important than a brand's level of quality. KISS, without the makeup, pyrotechnics, and alter-egos, is just another indistinguishable hard rock band, no matter how talented they may be.

KISS created a compelling enough difference in their unique look and sound that it didn't matter if they were virtuoso musicians or not. It could have been scientifically demonstrated over and over again that they weren't, and it wouldn't have slowed down their success. What did eventually slow down the KISS train was their decision to stop being different. As the band's late-1970s reign started to fade, they decided to abandon their makeup and costumes. In September 1983, they launched their new album *Lick It Up* and appeared publicly for the first time without makeup. In the short term, the novelty of a mask- and costume-free KISS was enough to generate renewed interest in the band, but that soon faded. The band spent several years struggling to find an identity and build their fan base. Without costumes and makeup, that challenge was amplified. KISS without makeup was simply another hard rock band with big hair. There was no longer anything to make KISS unique and interesting. Songs like "Lick It Up" and "Heaven's on Fire" were solid hits, but they couldn't sustain interest in a band that looked and sounded like every other 1980s hair band.

As is often the case, about twenty years after their debut, a sense of nostalgia built up around their brand. A generation of fans had now matured on their music, and as adults, they once again wanted the KISS they grew up with. A tribute album of artists performing KISS songs was released, with artists as diverse as Lenny Kravitz and Garth Brooks singing their own versions of the KISS songs that influenced them. Wisely, KISS tapped into the budding nostalgia and decided to return to makeup and mount a full-scale comeback in their original costumes and lineup. The result was fantastic. KISS was the top-selling concert act in 1996, and since putting the makeup back on, the band has enjoyed nonstop success touring around the world. That success isn't likely to stop anytime soon as the band continues to provide a show unlike any other night after night.

Recently inducted into the Rock and Roll Hall of Fame, rock star Alice Cooper is another fantastic example of the value of being different. When Alice Cooper started out in rock 'n' roll, he intentionally sought to build an image that ran counter to what everyone expected. While most rock stars positioned themselves as heroes, Alice Cooper created an onstage persona based on the concept of an antihero. Cooper took to the stage dressed as an androgynous witch, complete with torn clothing and black makeup. Cooper knew that by being dramatically different from every other aspiring rock star out there, he would get the attention that could launch his career. And launch his career it did.

Over the ensuing decades, Alice Cooper stood up as a rock 'n' roll original. Yes, he is a talented musician, no question. But what really set Alice Cooper apart is that he looked, acted, and sounded like no one else. Alice Cooper stood out because he was unique. Had he not stood out in the crowd, would anyone have had the chance to recognize his musical talent?

As the years went on, Alice Cooper continued to go

against the grain. His onstage image and elaborate theatrical antics never went away, but off the stage he did things his own way. He became a passionate golfer and born-again Christian, two traits not normally associated with long-haired, makeup-wearing rock stars. He helped other musicians recover from their battles with alcohol and drugs. While most rock stars attempt to portray a wild and crazy image, Cooper revels in his down-to-earth role. When the British newspaper *Sunday Times* asked him about reconciling his faith with his status as a rock star, Cooper said "Drinking beer is easy. Trashing your hotel room is easy. But being a Christian, that's a tough call. That's real rebellion!"

BATTLE OF THE GAMING CONSOLES: DIFFERENT BEATS BETTER

It may seem premature to look at video game consoles in an historical perspective, but the digital world moves at astounding speed. Video game consoles entered what is referred to as the "seventh generation" with the rise of the Xbox 360, Sony Playstation 3, and Nintendo Wii. These three consoles represent the bulk of the home video game market today.

Microsoft was the first on the scene, building the Xbox 360 on the success of their original Xbox platform. A year later both the Sony Playstation 3 (PS3) and the Nintendo Wii came out, giving the Xbox 360 some stiff competition. The PS3 and Xbox 360 share some similarities both visually and in terms of function. Both are similar-looking boxes controlled by similar-looking wireless remote control units.

The remotes for both include similar joysticks, triggers, and control surfaces. Competition between the two platforms seems to center on each console's graphic capabilities, the ability to immerse the gamer into the experience, and the availability of exclusive games such as the *Halo* series for Xbox 360 and the *Gran Turismo* driving games for Playstation 3.

Nintendo decided to take a completely different approach. The Wii console doesn't look anything like an Xbox 360 or a Sony Playstation 3. The remote controls look completely different and accessories like the "Nunchuks" are unlike anything Microsoft or Sony uses. The system lacks the graphic abilities of the Xbox 360 and the Playstation 3. Wii doesn't support DVDs, like Xbox 360, or Blu-Ray like the Sony Playstation 3. While the Microsoft and Sony platforms perform in high definition, the Nintendo Wii doesn't. The Wii doesn't even attempt to compete on those levels.

Instead, Nintendo created a console that reacts to the actions of the gamer. The unusual system integrates the motions of the user into the on-screen characters, allowing people to play games like tennis, bowling, and boxing using real physical movements. This represented an entirely new step in gaming and allowed the Wii to present itself as an entirely new type of gaming system. Any comparisons to Xbox 360 and Sony Playstation 3 were stifled because the Wii was so *different.*

The new system has opened up a previously untapped market for video games, including families, older consumers, fitness buffs, physical therapy centers, hospitals, and very young children. Instead of attempting to be better than Xbox 360 and Playstation 3, Nintendo took the approach of being different. Satoru Iwata, the president of Nintendo, declared that Nintendo wasn't "thinking about fighting Sony, but about how many people we can get to play games."

Nintendo's different approach has paid off. While Xbox 360 has sold more than 50 million units and Playstation 3 has moved more than 41 million consoles, Wii sales have exceeded 76 million! In Europe, Wii outsells Xbox 360 and Playstation 3 combined. Meanwhile, in Japan, Wii has sold more than 10 million consoles compared to about 5 million for Playstation 3 and only 1.2 million for Xbox 360.

Wii is the worldwide leader in home gaming systems, not because it is inherently better, but because it is special. Products that are "different" almost always beat products that are "better."

A Rock Star Five-Step Program:
How KISS Was Dramatically Different

1. **Makeup and costumes.** Sure David Bowie and others had worn glamorous makeup before, but until KISS walked onstage with painted faces and elaborate costumes, nobody had ever seen anything quite like it before.

2. **Their story.** KISS wasn't just about random makeup and costumes. Each member of the band had a comic book alter-ego. Each member of the band was part of a greater story.

3. **Fire, blood, and stage antics.** They blew stuff up on stage. Gene Simmons spit blood. And plenty of guitars were smashed. KISS didn't just play a concert; they gave their fans a show they would never forget.

4. **Controversy.** From the font that brought Nazi comparisons to the theory that KISS was an acronym for Knights In Satan's Service, KISS embraced the controversy every step of the way. They fed off of it.

5. **Commercialism.** From the beginning, the band was comfortable with their brand being displayed everywhere. While some bands fought the use of their logo and name to sell products, KISS encouraged it.

CHAPTER SEVENTEEN

ABBA-FY YOUR BRAND

Quite possibly the smartest branding advice I've ever heard a rock star give came from Björn Ulvaeus of ABBA when he described why the band would never get back together and appear onstage again, despite persistent offers of millions of dollars to reunite:

> *We would like people to remember us as we were. Young, exuberant, full of energy and ambition. I remember Robert Plant saying Led Zeppelin was a cover band now because they cover all their own stuff. I think that hit the nail on the head.*

So many bands, and brands, neglect this incredibly important concept: It doesn't matter what you think you are. All that matters is what your customers and fans think you are.

Flashing back to chapter one, AC/DC demonstrated how consistency is a pillar to building a great brand, and how being consistent buys you a piece of mental "real estate" in the minds of your customers. That mental real estate is extremely limited space (think Manhattan), and you are lucky to have it! While you, the business owner or manager, lives and breathes your product, it is often forgotten that your customers have a million other things on their mind. They don't have a lot of space leftover in their brains to think about your product. If you've been fortunate enough to establish a place in the mind of the customer, you need to not only respect it—you need to worship it, like ABBA continues to do more than thirty years after they last played together.

ABBA did a wonderful job of selling to the world a brand that was young, exuberant, and full of energy and ambition. They made music that was unique and fresh. If they reunited today, could the sixty-five-year-old Ulvaeus lead the band with the same vigor? Could they make music that was unique and fresh? Of course not, and their fans wouldn't want to hear unique and fresh music. Their fans would want to hear the ABBA hits from the 1970s.

Since ABBA cannot possibly give their fans the youth and vigor that made the band famous, they steadfastly refuse to reunite. They do a brilliant job of keeping their brand alive through consistent rereleases of their numerous greatest hits collections and by their involvement in *Mamma Mia!* onstage and in film. But through it all they continue to spurn all offers to reunite. Rumor is that the offers have been massive, as much as one BILLION dollars to play a hundred concerts. That's commitment!

Photo credit: Photofest

ABBA refuses to reunite because they feel they could never deliver on or live up to the expectations of their fans.

ABBA can serve as a model for brands in terms of focus. ABBA remains focused on being the band that their fans remember, but many businesses lack the commitment to focus on exactly what their customers want from them.

If you are able to convince a significant number of people in your community that your business is the one to call for in-house computer repairs, think about focusing on that and shutting down your brick-and-mortar location. Put all your energy into having your technicians visit customers in their homes. If your are able to convince a significant number of people in your community that your store is the best place to get high-end shoes, focus on the exclusive stuff and drop all low-end shoes from your inventory. Stop having sales. Raise prices, raise service levels, and make shopping in your store a true experience.

If you are able to convince a significant number of people in your community that your restaurant is the best place for breakfast, focus on breakfast. Consider serving breakfast twenty-four hours a day (and nothing else) or closing up at 11 a.m. and leaving the lunch crowd to all of the other restaurants. But for the love of ABBA, don't start marketing your dinner menu!

Logic seems to always lead us in the opposite direction. We focus on the areas of our business where we are weak, instead of where we are strong. Rock star brands, like ABBA, focus on strengths. What do our fans think we are great at? What do we need to stop doing in order to be better at that?

How can your brand be more like ABBA, without applying for a Swedish passport?

First, find out what your customers think you are. What *you* think you are matters very little. Research your customers, engage them in dialogue, and understand what piece of mental real estate you've managed to carve out. Always remember that you are defined by what they think you are, not what you think you are. Monitor the conversations happening about you. Doing that has never been easier, thanks to social media. Google can be set to automatically update you when your brand is mentioned in online discussions. Quick searches on Twitter and Facebook can turn up a wealth of information about what your customers think about your brand. Smart brands engage their customers in discussion, and get to know what their fans think they are doing right and wrong.

Once you know what your fans expect of you, build your strategy around that mental real estate and focus on demonstrating to more and more people how great that real estate is. Don't lose sight and try to acquire more real estate, but instead work hard to drive more people to the valuable mental real estate you are fortunate enough to already own. Remember that with each step you take toward acquiring more mental real estate, you potentially risk losing the mental real estate you already owned.

Finally, be grateful that you own any mental real estate at all. It is hard to come by. Some brands spend their entire existence fighting to own even the tiniest slice of it, and they never get there. If you've convinced a group of people that you are great at something, celebrate it!

Remember that your piece of mental real estate doesn't need to be huge to be hugely rewarding. Many brands have become incredibly large thanks to a very small idea. Facebook was a very small idea when Mark Zuckerberg started it as a Harvard-based social networking site in the winter of 2004. It wasn't long before that very small idea got bigger, as Zuckerberg opened it up to students at other Boston-area schools, then Ivy League schools, Stanford, and soon college campuses all over North America. Within two years, Facebook was accessible to everyone over the age of thirteen. Today it ranks as one of the Internet's most heavily used websites and continues to grow. Facebook would never have grown as rapidly as it did if it wasn't a concept with tremendous singular focus.

A Rock Star Five-Step Program: Landmark Albums ABBA's Greatest Hits Has Outsold

You may be surprised just how big the ABBA brand remains. Their greatest hits album *Abba Gold* has sold 28 million copies. Here are five albums that ABBA has outsold:

1. *Never Mind* by Nirvana (26 million copies)

2. *Greatest Hits* by Queen (25 million)

3. *The Joshua Tree* by U2 (25 million)

4. *Legend: Greatest Hits* by Bob Marley & The Wailers (20 million)

5. *Purple Rain* by Prince (20 million)

▼

CHAPTER EIGHTEEN

KNOW YOUR ENEMY: GREEN DAY MEETS SUN TZU

I was driving home one warm summer evening, windows down, sunglasses on, and the radio cranked. It was a perfect ending to a busy day, and I had found the perfect sound track to go with it: the Green Day song "Know Your Enemy." Nothing says "I'm done with work" like the anarchy of Green Day! But the song title poses an interesting challenge for brands. Do you know your enemy?

While the bulk of a brand's focus should always be on its own customers, it is also vital to know and understand your enemy. Rock star brands know their enemy. They not only know who the enemy is, but they know what he stands for, and how he will react to what they do.

Green Day performs on *Saturday Night Live* in 2009.

Without Lex Luther, there is no need for Superman.

Without Goliath, there is no need for David.

Without Demons, there is no need for Angels.

In branding, the same holds true. When you stand for something meaningful, there will always be someone who stands for the opposite. If your brand is built on amazing customer service, your enemy might be the low-price company that you compete against. If your brand's foundation is fast delivery, your enemy could be the company that specializes in customized products. Whatever the case, you have an enemy and you need him. You need your enemy. Sound crazy?

Pepsi needs Coke. Sure, they want you to drink their cola instead of Coke. But without Coke to position as "old," Pepsi could never position their brand as "young."

Apple needs Microsoft. If there were no Microsoft, there would be no Mac vs. PC ads, which so beautifully sum up the philosophical differences between the two brands.

The Yankees need the Red Sox. Sure, they want to beat

them and they certainly want to knock them out come playoff time. But would the American League be better without a Sox-Yankees rivalry? Those rivalries help sell millions of dollars in tickets, beer, and merchandise every season. Hating each other is a major part of what defines these two brands.

Having a clear and defined position in the market is critical. So is having a clear and defined *opposition*. Your position lets everyone on your team know what you stand for. Your opposition tells your team, and the world, what you stand against. That doesn't mean you need to embark on a negative marketing blitz. It simply means that to clearly define your brand, it helps to understand which brands stand for the opposite ideals that you represent.

Home Depot, now with nearly 2,300 stores, is America's largest home-improvement store. They've exploded since opening in 1978 by creating large warehouse-style stores that dwarfed their traditional competitors. Lowe's had already been around for fifty-seven years when Home Depot opened their first store, but like nearly every other home improvement store they quickly found themselves victimized by Home Depot's big-box style stores. Lowe's countered Home Depot by looking for an opposite position. They found it in gender.

While Home Depot stores were large, dusty, and intimidating, Lowe's made their stores clean and bright. They began to attract a new crowd of shoppers that was less experienced in home-improvement projects, including a wealth of female customers who wouldn't set foot in a Home Depot store. This "know your enemy" approach gained Lowe's a strong position in the market. Even though they remain the number two home-improvement retailer, they are also the fastest-growing home-improvement store.

Another retail battle, Walmart versus Target, illustrates the "know your enemy" approach clearly. Walmart is legendary for their relentless pursuit of low prices. They have revolutionized their own systems and the systems of their many suppliers by demanding across-the-board consistency to reduce costs. Their marketing focus is laser-sharp, aimed squarely at offering the lowest prices possible. How can you take on a competitor who is that zealous about undercutting your prices? You know your enemy.

Target found the inherent opposite in Walmart's low-price strategy: quality and fashion. If your primary focus is low price, it is impossible to simultaneously position your brand as high quality. You simply can't own both images. Target has thrived for years by offering slightly more upscale, trend-forward merchandise. They design their stores to be more attractive than Walmart by offering wider aisles, improved merchandise display, and a focus on the in-store environment. The result is that Target attracts the youngest consumer of any major department store, with a median age of forty-one. Their customers are not only younger, but also more affluent. Walmart remains the largest discount retailer in America (and the world's largest public corporation), but Target has solidified their position as number two with an attractive customer base and strong point of differentiation. They clearly know their enemy.

Everywhere you look you can find brands that know their enemy.

Disneyland represents the perfect family getaway to a world where everything is perfect and magical. On the other hand, Las Vegas represents an adult escape to a place where anything goes, no matter how sinful, and nobody will ever tell on you.

Rolex has been the ultimate luxury watch for decades. James Bond wore a Rolex. In recent years, Breitling has positioned themselves as the watch of choice among professional explorers, pilots, navigators, and sea captains. Rolex remains the watch of the boardroom, but Breitling has become the watch of the cockpit.

Defining your enemy becomes even more important when you are launching a new brand and attempting to build a new product category. Southwest Airlines created the low-cost airline concept to gain a foothold in the airline industry. They did so by establishing what they weren't. They weren't going to have first class cabins, meals on planes, reserved seat assignments, or multiple types of aircraft. All of those things became enemies of their number one mission: to be the low-cost carrier.

Chipotle Mexican Grill has quickly become a rock star brand by establishing what it stands against. Chipotle is against frozen foods. None of the restaurants have a microwave oven or a freezer. Chipotle stands against unethical treatment of animals and uses naturally raised meat, organic produce, and hormone-free dairy per their "Food with Integrity" mission statement. By clearly stating what they are against, Chipotle has not only become one of the fastest growing and most successful fast-food chains, but it has done so by creating a new product category—healthy, responsible, and fast Mexican food.

What you stand against matters just as much as what you stand for. Rock star brands know themselves well and know their enemies equally well. They understand what separates them from the competition and how to use those differences to win. There is nothing new about this lesson. Sun Tzu recognized it in chapter three of *The Art of War*:

> *So it is said that if you know your enemies and know yourself, you can win a hundred battles without a single loss. If you only know yourself, but not your opponent, you may win or may lose. If you know neither yourself nor your enemy, you will always endanger yourself.*

Would you think that Green Day, a punk band that played Woodstock '94 covered in mud, could channel the lessons of a great Chinese philosopher?

A Rock Star Five-Step Program: Modern Brand Enemies

While much of what is discussed in this chapter happens subtly and below the radar of the average consumer, some famous branding battles have taken on very public profiles. Sometimes that profile is because of the sheer size of the companies involved, and sometimes it is thanks to advertisements that directly attack the competition. Here are five modern branding battles:

1. **Pepsi vs. Coke.** These two have been going at it for years and probably always will be. Pepsi has created some very memorable ads that directly attack Coke. However, Diet Coke's recent surge into the number two spot in cola sales may change the nature of this battle.

2. **Lowe's vs. Home Depot.** As profiled earlier in chapter eighteen, this battle centers around each brand's image. Home Depot is the category leader, but upstart Lowe's has established a reputation based on a "friendlier" image.

3. **Apple vs. Microsoft/Dell.** Apple has outwardly mocked the PC (and most obviously Microsoft) in their Mac vs. PC ads. The award-winning campaign painted PC users as handcuffed by ineffective and impersonal software.

4. **Target vs. Walmart.** Target has grown quickly because of their ability to position themselves as an upscale store compared to Walmart. It goes beyond marketing. Their stores have a look and feel that conveys this same image.

5. **FOX News vs. CNN.** FOX took on longtime leader CNN by appealing to an audience seeking opinion and entertainment as much as news. They have successfully packaged

continued on following page

entertainment programs as news programming, and in
doing so, they have taken down CNN as the market leader
in cable news.

▼

CHAPTER NINETEEN

CHANGE WITH THE TIMES: EMINEM'S COMEBACK

Marshall Mathers was a revolutionary figure in the explosive growth of hip-hop music. In the early 2000s, he—under the name Eminem—emerged as the genre's biggest star and brought together black and white musicians in a way previous hip-hop stars hadn't done before. Eminem drew comparisons to Elvis Presley, who fifty years earlier did the same thing with soul, R&B, and country to help create what we know today as rock 'n' roll.

Many of Eminem's early hits were part social commentary, part sketch comedy, and part music. Songs like "The Real Slim Shady," "My Band," and "Without Me" were as humorous as they were biting. Much of what Eminem had to say in those early days was about himself, and much of it was boastful and self-promoting. It was fun music at the time, and it did very, very well. Between 2000 and 2005, Eminem sold nearly 40 million albums.

But over the next few years, those self-important, insincere Eminem songs faded away. His stardom seemed to fade too, and his 2009 album *Relapse* sold just 3 million copies, a far cry from expectations. By 2009, Eminem was written off by many as an important figure in music history but no longer a relevant artist.

Photo credit: Photofest

Eminem's early hits lacked the honesty and authenticity that fans find in his newer music.

Cue the comeback music. In 2010, Eminem once again owned pop music. His album, *Recovery*, spawned hit after hit. He was a guest voice on several of the year's biggest songs. Seemingly overnight, Eminem went from being written off to being written up by *Billboard* magazine as the artist of the year. What changed?

In 2010, Eminem tapped into an undeniable social shift toward a more civic era, and away from the self-centered idealist era. Instead of boastful songs about himself, Eminem sang about finding luck and good fortune in the song "Airplanes" by B.o.B. featuring Hayley Williams. His duet with Rihanna, "I Love the Way You Lie," touched a nerve with anyone who has ever been in a passionate relationship, and the song competed with "Airplanes" as one of the year's biggest hits. On his own, Eminem addressed his personal insecurities, drug rehab, and relationships. He had been through a lot in the previous few years, and those challenges had a definite impact on the songs he chose for the album and the passion with which he performed them. *Recovery* revealed an Eminem that was a lot like the rest of us, and his message resonated in a major way.

To a lesser degree, the same thing happened with another hip-hop star from the same era, Nelly. His early-2000s hits like "Ride wit Me" and "Hot in Herre" were massive hits that were driven by lyrics about Nelly and his greatness. After several years without any appearances on the charts, Nelly also returned in a big way in 2010. His number one hit "Just a Dream" was a much more personal and intimate song that revealed vulnerabilities that his fans hadn't heard him sing about in his earlier music. The charts in 2010 looked a lot like 2003 thanks to Eminem and Nelly and their newfound sense of honesty.

Bestselling author and speaker Roy Williams has written and blogged extensively at MondayMorningMemo.com about his theory of a forty-year pendulum. This pendulum, Williams suggests, takes North American society on a regular journey from self-focused idealist eras to community-driven civic eras. This journey takes almost exactly forty years. According to Williams, these changes can clearly be observed in popular culture through the decades. If what Williams theorizes is true, Eminem had no choice. It was either become honest and real or become irrelevant and fade away. And this concept doesn't just apply to rappers, it applies to brands and the messages they use to communicate with their customers.

In 2010, Pepsi embarked on a promotion called "Refresh." The campaign doesn't reward any Pepsi drinkers with free bottles of soda or trips or cash. Instead, Pepsi asks people to suggest ways to make their communities better places. They will then choose various initiatives to improve communities and "change the world," funding them with up to $250,000. Nothing about this promotion communicates anything boastful about Pepsi. There are no claims to great taste. That stuff doesn't connect with people as well during a civic cycle the way a mission to improve our parks, streets, schools, and safety does. Is the "Refresh" campaign generating sales for Pepsi? At this point we don't know, but it is absolutely tapping into our evolving, civic-minded way of thinking.

An interesting example of this shift in thinking is a recent campaign used by several orthodontists and dentists around the country. The "Candy Buy-Back" program offers gift cards and other rewards to children in exchange for their Halloween candy. The focus is on candy that can damage orthodontic appliances. The repurchased candy is then shipped to US troops serving overseas to show support. The buy-back campaign doesn't generate immediate sales, but it does offer a fantastic PR opportunity that allows a local business to show how they are striving to make their community better. That's a huge benefit in an increasingly civic-minded society.

A Rock Star Five-Step Program: Building Civic-Minded Marketing

1. **Stop bragging.** Being boastful doesn't connect anymore. If you want to prove to customers that you are the best at what you do, use proof and allow your customers to experience your brand's brilliance for themselves.

2. **Expose your cracks.** In a civic-minded society, we are more accepting of flaws, and we better understand that all of us have them. Brands willing to expose their imperfections connect with people on a deeper level.

3. **Word-of-mouth rules.** With a single click, your customers can let their friends and family know how great (or how bad) your brand is. You can't hide from bad service any longer.

4. **Honesty rocks.** Customers today are armed with an incredible ability to detect BS. The younger your target customers are, the more sensitive their BS-detector will be. If you set off their detector, you lose.

5. **Belonging is the key.** Today's American dream isn't about beating everyone else on your way to the top. It is more about being a vital part of a productive team.

▼

CHAPTER TWENTY

THE NOT-SO-DIRE STRAITS OF CONTROVERSY

Mark Knopfler didn't plan to insult the gay community when he wrote "Money for Nothing" in 1985. He was at a furniture store and overheard the guys moving furniture complaining about how rock stars get rich without trying. They bemoaned that rock stars "get their money for nothing and their chicks for free" while they had to "move these refrigerators . . . these color TVs." The result was an iconic rock song that won a Grammy for "Best Rock Performance by a Duo or Group" at the 1985 Grammy Awards. It topped the charts in the United States for three weeks that year, and the groundbreaking animated video became the first video ever played on MTV Europe.

All of that happened despite some initial controversy over the lyrics. Several lines in the song were labeled racist ("banging on the bongos like a chimpanzee"), sexist ("chicks for free"), and homophobic ("little faggot with the earring and the makeup"). The band released an edited version of the song that eliminated some of the offensive words and shortened up its epic 8:26 run time to a more radio-friendly length, but the unedited original continued to be a staple of classic rock stations around the world without any additional controversy.

All of that changed in January 2011 when the Canadian government ruled that the use of the word "faggot" constituted a breach of the Canadian Broadcast Standards Council code of ethics. That decision, initiated by a single complaint from a radio listener in St. John's, Newfoundland, resulted in Canadian radio stations being effectively banned from playing the unedited original song without potentially facing repercussions. Twenty-six years after the song first became a hit, it was suddenly thrust into headlines around the world.

With the wildfire spread of the story on social networks and mainstream media, the song became one of Canada's most-downloaded songs on the iTunes chart. Nearly thirty years after it was released as the world's first CD-single, the digital version acquired a new lease on life. Thousands of people paid ninety-nine cents each to make "Money for Nothing" a part of their musical collection and to hear what all the fuss was about, putting the band Dire Straits back on the charts alongside Eminem and Taylor Swift and other 2011 contemporaries.

At the time of the Dire Straits incident, I was overseeing content for nearly eighty radio stations across Canada. Most of them had not played "Money for Nothing" with any regularity for years. It was just one of those lost 1980s classics that popped up every now and then. In the years leading up to 2011, very few listeners called our radio stations asking to hear "Money for Nothing." Suddenly, after this decision was made public, hundreds of listeners were calling to request the song and voice their opinion. By electing to continue to play the unedited version of the song, our radio stations became instant folk heroes to listeners who spoke out in staggering numbers in support of free speech! The overwhelming majority of listeners, both gay and straight, were of the opinion that suppression of free speech was a far greater risk than the offense caused by the contextual use of the word "faggot" in "Money for Nothing." Even those bothered by the lyric were generally grateful for the discussion that the controversy created.

Dire Straits hadn't had a significant hit since the early 1990s, and the band broke up in 1995. Unexpectedly and after years of relative obscurity, they were once again on the charts thanks to the power of a good controversy. Most of the time, controversy is considered a negative. *Wikipedia* defines it as "a state of prolonged public dispute or debate, usually concerning a matter of opinion." Based on that definition, most brands wisely try to avoid controversy. But as

Dire Straits saw in 2011, in certain circumstances, a controversy can be a great thing for a brand.

Calvin Klein is a brand built on sex. Klein himself once stated "Jeans are about sex," and the brand's advertising has reflected that belief. It began with fifteen-year-old Brooke Shields saying, "Want to know what's between me and my Calvin's? Nothing." Since then, their ads have not only featured revealing and suggestive images, but they have also blurred the lines of age, sexual orientation, and even gender identity. They have consistently been the target of complaints, yet they continue to be a very successful clothing brand.

One of the most notorious instances was in 1995 when Calvin Klein used teenaged models in provocative poses selling underwear and jeans. Child protection groups protested and the US Department of Justice began to investigate the company for possibly violating federal child pornography and exploitation laws. The company pulled the ads, but not before their jeans became the must-have item of the year. As one anonymous marketing director at the time said, this controversy took Klein's "coolness factor from a ten to a sixty." Calvin Klein didn't stop their sexually suggestive advertising because of those concerns. Since then they have continued to push the envelope in their advertising, and they continue to be the subject of frequent complaints. Those complaints only serve to make their brand identity stronger.

Red Bull has been beaten up many times. In 2009, Red Bull exported from Austria was discovered to contain trace amounts of cocaine. A 2008 study reported that drinking even one can of Red Bull had a negative impact on blood coagulation and raised the risk of having a heart attack. The drink was even banned in France, Norway, and Denmark, although the bans have since been lifted in Norway and Denmark. Athletes, especially young athletes, have been cautioned by health organizations against using Red Bull to hydrate or to increase performance. Today, despite all of the concerns, Red Bull is the most popular energy drink in the world thanks in large part to the massive amount of publicity that they generated by being a controversial product.

On the other hand, the list of brands that have been damaged a great deal by controversy is long.

Tiger Woods' brand value will never be the same after his sex scandal in 2009. He may have been the best golfer in the world, but his image, and so far his golf game, will never recover because of the depth of the scandal.

British Petroleum will have a difficult challenge ahead after the 2010 Gulf of Mexico oil spill. They had spent the decade leading up to the spill forging an image of a more environmentally aware oil company, but all of that work was undone by the Gulf spill.

Union Carbide will forever be connected with the instant deaths of 3,800 people in Bhopal, India. Even though Union Carbide effectively gave birth to the modern petrochemical industry, any good brand image they had was heavily damaged on that December night in 1984 when gas leaked from their Indian plant.

Gary Glitter, despite having one of rock's most famous cheer-along songs with "Rock 'n' Roll Part 2," has his name inextricably linked to child abuse. His three drunk-driving convictions in the 1980s didn't kill his career, but his eventual arrest for possessing child pornography did. He fled from the United Kingdom and lived for short periods in various countries including Colombia, Cuba, Venezuela, Thailand, and eventually Cambodia. He was later deported to Vietnam to face charges of child abuse for having sexual relations with girls as young as ten and eleven. After serving prison time, Glitter was denied entry in at least nineteen countries before deciding to return to England to attempt to live in obscurity for fear of hostility toward him.

Certainly nothing good can come to any brand that destroys the environment, kills innocent people, lies to the public, and abuses children. There's just no hidden upside in such extreme controversy.

CALVIN KLEIN'S BRIEF HISTORY OF CONTROVERSY

1980: A fifteen-year-old Brooke Shields tells the world that "nothing comes between me and my Calvin's." The use of a model so young and a caption so provocative was certainly controversial at the time. However, the ads helped establish Calvin Klein as the leader in this massive designer jeans category.

1993: Kate Moss appears in Calvin Klein ads looking gaunt. Her grunge-influenced, waif-like appearance generates tremendous discussion about eating disorders and the model's own health, and prompts President Bill Clinton to comment on the growing "heroin-chic" look among young women.

1995: The much talked about campaign appears in which extremely young-looking models of both genders cavort in their underwear in a suburban room that resembles a 1970s porn set. The justice department investigates, but no charges are ever levied, and the ads are taken down.

1999: Instead of employing teenagers, Calvin Klein turns to young child models to launch a new line of children's underwear. Boys and girls are photographed in their underwear playing on a sofa. The ads are placed in Times Square, and in the *New York Post* and other prominent magazines. The ads lasted only twenty-four hours before being pulled due to public uproar.

2009: Calvin Klein placed a 50-foot billboard in New York's Times Square that featured what appeared to be a scantily clad foursome engaged in sexual acts. The ads once again sparked outrage and debate.

A Rock Star Five-Step Program: How Controversy Can Benefit a Brand

1. **When the controversy speaks to the brand's image.** Calvin Klein fashions are all about sex, so generating controversy over sexually suggestive ads is perfectly in line with the brand's image. Red Bull is most popular with young, edgy consumers who thrive on danger. Controversy that positions Red Bull as dangerous is perfect for the brand's image.

2. **When the controversy doesn't (directly) hurt anyone.** The impact of hearing Dire Straits say "faggot" isn't instantly measurable and is certainly up for debate. Viewing suggestive Calvin Klein ads might be detrimental to someone, but it is impossible to determine exactly who and how. Red Bull might be dangerous, but it has only been indirectly linked to deaths, such as a 2009 instance where a twenty-one-year-old woman died after drinking four cans of Red Bull. But the drinks were mixed with alcohol, and it was later determined that she had a rare heart condition and epilepsy. As long as there is no direct link, it is unlikely to hurt the Red Bull brand.

3. **When the controversy is temporary.** Soon we'll forget about the "Money for Nothing" lyrics again. Calvin Klein ads will be taken down and new ones put up. Some future research will probably show that Red Bull is safe enough. For all of these brands, controversies will probably come and go and come again. While controversy is good for each of these brands, it cannot be the only thing driving them forward. They can thrive on temporary controversy,

but seldom can controversy form a brand's primary directive. You can't build many successful long-term brands on controversy alone.

4. **When public opinion is likely to be on your side.** Some things, like overt political correctness, can galvanize people around your brand. Pepsi ran an ad during the 2011 Super Bowl that created a racial-stereotyping controversy that bordered on "PC-Gone-Wild," and public sentiment was in their favor. If you sense that public opinion will largely be on your side, riding a little wave of controversy in order to maximize buzz about your brand might just be the right thing to do. Quite often your fans and customers will rally to your defense if they sense that your brand is the subject of unfair criticism.

5. **When your story is solid.** Oscar Wilde famously said "The only thing worse than being talked about is not being talked about." If a controversy erupts around your brand, you can seize the moment and use the opportunity to tell your solid and engaging story. In the 1990s, embroiled in a scandal about purchasing diamonds from countries run by controversial leaders, De Beers used the spotlight to create a new certification process to determine the origin of all diamonds and publicly state their plan to stop inadvertently supporting these regimes. In the end, the attention probably benefited their brand.

Handled properly, a controversy can be a great thing for a brand. For the right brand at the right time, it can quickly help build brand identity, create excitement, raise awareness, and move products.

▼

CHAPTER TWENTY-ONE

THE GRATEFUL DEAD'S CRYSTAL BALL

Nobody can predict the future. Trends emerge and fade. Fashions come and go. Musical styles evolve and change. Along the way, great bands—and great brands—rise and fall.

But in the late 1960s and early 1970s, one band appears to have seen the future. Considering the number of hallucinogens they were taking, it is quite possible that the Grateful Dead certainly saw *something*, and it probably wasn't the future. But what The Dead did do was create a business model that looks surprisingly like the music industry we see and hear today.

Thank the LSD, warm California air, or call it pure genius, but the Grateful Dead innovated numerous concepts that are even today considered cutting-edge for many brands.

Photo credit: Photofest

The late Jerry Garcia and the Grateful Dead built up a social network long before the term even existed.

File sharing: Almost four decades before Napster, Limewire, Bit Torrent, and YouTube, the Grateful Dead started encouraging their fans to record their concerts and share them with other fans. They believed that if they allowed this previously illegal act to happen, their music would spread virally. They understood that whatever they lost in potential concert ticket and album sales, they would make up ten times over in passionate fans. The band even created a special section at their concerts for "tapers" to get the best possible results. To this day, trading and collecting tapes of Grateful Dead concerts is incredibly popular and made even more feasible thanks to the Internet.

At the time, the music industry thought this practice was insane. How could you give away your product like that? If you gave away recordings of your concerts, why would anybody come to your shows in the future? The Grateful Dead knew better. They knew that if they allowed their music to spread virally, they would develop a larger and more passionate fan base. Newly converted fans would be the ones lined up for tickets the next time the band came to town.

Database marketing: Even in today's connected world with easy access to e-mail and SMS messaging, some brands are living in the past when it comes to database marketing. Yet the Grateful Dead started building their database in 1971 when they placed a note inside their *Skull & Roses* album asking fans to send in their mailing addresses so they could keep in touch. The band began to communicate with these fans regularly, never selling any unwanted things to them. It was a simple and powerful way to get to know their fans, and to let their fans get to know them.

Fan clubs weren't a new thing, but the Grateful Dead took it pretty seriously. They sent out regular newsletters to these people and periodically sent them gifts and sneak previews of music they were working on. The Dead realized that if they developed a strong network of fans—a community or tribe as we would call it today—they would have a built-in audience to buy tickets to their next concert tour.

Social causes: Years before recycling and carbon offsetting were vogue, the Grateful Dead handed out garbage bags at their shows to lessen the environmental impact. Jerry Garcia and Bob Weir spoke to the United Nations in September 1988 about the harvesting of the rainforests, and introduced a partnership with the Rainforest Action Network to raise money and awareness.

These causes were part of the Grateful Dead's image because they mattered to the band, and the band wasn't afraid to tell people what mattered to them. Today celebrities making political endorsements and taking a stand on social issues is common, but back then it wasn't. The Grateful Dead popularized the concept of using celebrity status to further important social causes.

Visual symbols: Like the iconic Nike "swoosh," the Grateful Dead created a series of visual cues that fans could identify with. They weren't formal logos, but rather icons that represented the band. The dancing bears, terrapins, jesters, and the famous red, white, and blue skull with the lightning bolt have all come to represent the band without any words or music. Those multiple visual symbols also created numerous merchandising opportunities. Today's sports teams are masters of creating alternate jerseys and retro-logos to capitalize on the revenue stream. They can thank the Grateful Dead for that.

Having visual symbols identifies you as a member of a community. Today, that might mean a logo on your Facebook page, but in the 1970s it wasn't so simple. Ancient Christians, fearing persecution from the Roman Empire, used the Ichthys fish symbol to quietly let others know who they were. In the same way, Dead Heads can use any number of symbols to let other Dead Heads know who they are.

A "Dead Head sticker on a Cadillac," as Don Henley sang in "The Boys of Summer," is a perfect example.

Merchandising: Nobody understood merchandising like The Dead. While other bands only supplemented their income with tour T-shirts, the Grateful Dead made millions from their brand. Years before bands like KISS turned merchandising into a way of life, the Grateful Dead were already on it.

It may seem counterintuitive based on their encouragement of bootlegging and the close relationship they maintained with their fans, but The Grateful Dead were pioneers in protecting their music and their intellectual rights. They were among the first artists to retain ownership of their merchandising rights, master tapes, and publishing rights. They retained their own legal counsel, a man named Hal Kant, for more than thirty-five years. Kant was so entrenched in the band's affairs that his Grateful Dead business card identified him as "Czar."

Love their music or not, you can't deny the visionary brilliance of the Grateful Dead. And for much of what they did, the experts at the time mocked them:

Fans recording concerts? Insane.
Database marketing? Hardly worth the trouble.
Social causes? That's for politicians.
Intellectual rights? The record company gets those.

Rock star brands don't always play by everyone else's

rules. They do things differently. They understand what matters to their fans and reflect that in how they do business. Rock star brands don't look to the past or to the crowd to see what they should do next; they set their own course for the future. They are revolutionary. When you embark on something revolutionary, you won't have any shortage of people telling you that you are wrong.

When you draw your own road map, you risk getting lost. You don't have the same GPS that others have. Yet by drawing your own road map, you might discover places and routes that others have never seen before. You might just find a new way to do things that will change the world. Only those willing to take the risk, as the Grateful Dead did, will ever know the rewards.

A Rock Star Five-Step Program: Carrying Forth the Dead's Philosophies

With Jerry Garcia's passing, the Grateful Dead ceased to be. But their influence permeates the music industry and will for generations. There are a number of bands today that have picked up the torch to carry their attitudes and ideals forward. Here are five of the most prominent. Note that I didn't include tribute acts, like Dark Star Orchestra, in this list:

1. **Phish.** The most widely known jam band got their start doing Grateful Dead covers. They grew into one of the most popular post-Dead jam bands.

2. **Moonalice.** Although their musical ties to the Dead are clear, they are probably the best example of how the Grateful Dead might be using social media if they were around today. Follow them on Twitter @Moonalice, and learn how they invented the Twittercast concert.

3. **RatDog.** The band was Dead member Bob Weir's side project, but became his full-time job when Jerry Garcia died. RatDog plays an eclectic mix of cover songs (from the Dead and others) and original tunes.

4. **Further.** Bob Weir and Phil Lesh, both Grateful Dead members, created Further in 2008. They actively tour today, drawing legions of Dead fans to their shows.

5. **Widespread Panic.** Like the Dead, Widespread Panic never plays the same set list twice. They also actively encourage fans to tape their shows and share the recordings.

6. **Honorable mention: Dave Matthews Band.** As jam-band as they are, they also have mainstream radio appeal that transcends anything the Dead ever had. Having commercial success puts them in a different genre than the Grateful Dead.

CHAPTER TWENTY-TWO

▼

THE ENCORE: APPLYING THE ROCK STAR PRINCIPLES

Every year, millions of people pick up a guitar for the first time and learn a few chords. They dream big, but the vast majority of them will never play in front of an audience. Even fewer will ever collect a paycheck for their efforts. Of those who eventually get paid, a slim few ever reach the elite status of rock star. Great bands, like great brands, are rare.

The odds of making it big are stacked against both musicians and entrepreneurs, yet that doesn't stop us from doing what we love. It is in our DNA, this need to create. While musicians create songs seemingly out of thin air, entrepreneurs create businesses from ideas in their heads. Both have the need to turn something imaginary into something tangible. Like aspiring rock stars who refuse to give up their dreams, entrepreneurs fight on through setbacks and failures to create products, businesses, and brands that become part of our collective lives. The world is a better place for it.

Putting the principles outlined in *Brand Like a Rock Star* into practice might seem daunting at first. But taken step by step, it is manageable. It turns out that starting a brand is just like starting a band.

STARTING YOUR BAND

It begins with a passion.

U2 was a group of high school friends who sang passionately about the politics and influences that shaped their lives growing up in Dublin, Ireland. As they rose to fame, they continued to sing passionately about the world around them.

Bob Marley's music didn't have a name when he started out. It was a sound, not a genre. As reggae took off and Bob Marley's legend grew, he continued to create passionate music about his country, his people, his religion, and his family.

Bruce Springsteen watched the America he loved start to divide socially over the Vietnam War. He watched small towns collapse in the economic crisis of the early 1970s. From those experiences, he created passionate songs about real people living real lives.

Great bands are founded on passion. When you create something out of a deep desire to change the world, people pay attention. You believe; we believe. Brands founded on passion have the same ability to capture our interest. Lululemon Athletica's founders passionately believe in the power of yoga. Ben & Jerry turned their hippie-era ideals into an ice cream empire. Companies like Whole Foods and Patagonia clothing were built on world-changing ideals in their respective product categories. Steve Jobs started Apple in a garage, with only a few hundred dollars and a passion for computers. For Richard Branson, the genesis for his multiplatform Virgin brand was his passion to find new ways to help people have a good time. That driving force has manifested itself in music, mobile, radio, aviation, and countless other areas where Virgin-branded products exist.

What do you believe in? How is it reflected in your product and your company? That root passion is where your rock star brand begins.

REHEARSALS

In the early days, things are tough for any young band. The Beatles spent the first few years of the 1960s playing long nights in the bars of Hamburg, Germany. Those were grueling years, with very little money and very little fame. But they were formative years, during which the band refined their formula, built up their skills, and developed their sound.

Bob Dylan was a college dropout living in Greenwich Village in New York City. He played coffeehouses and clubs

in the city, slowly building a network of friends and followers that would eventually help launch his career.

The business world is no different. There are very few
Facebook-style overnight success stories to tell. Most rock
star brands began very small and grew relatively slowly. Nike
was a little company called Blue Ribbon Sports that University of Oregon track athlete Phil Knight founded in 1964.
Knight sold an obscure brand of Japanese shoes out of the
trunk of his car. It was two years before they established an
actual retail store, and fourteen years before the company
changed its name to Nike.

Starbucks' lowly beginnings go back to 1971 and a single
retail location in Seattle, where they sold high-end coffee
beans, tea, and spices. They didn't even make coffee or sell
muffins, scones, and sandwiches. It took eleven years until the
idea of actually making coffee and espresso was considered.
Sixteen years after that, they started to expand rapidly.

The Simpsons spent three years as a short sketch on *The
Tracey Ullman Show* before being developed into a half-hour
prime-time show for FOX-TV. It became the network's first
show to crack the Nielsen ratings and it enhanced Fox's credibility. But *The Simpsons* needed those three years to find its
identity.

Every band, and brand, needs that incubation time to
refine their craft. Lennon and McCartney needed to figure
out how to write songs together. Bob Dylan needed to meet
Woody Guthrie and immerse himself in the folk counterculture of Greenwich Village.

Has your brand had that valuable incubation time to grow and develop? Have you run prototypes and demo versions and rough copies past your trusted colleagues and friends?

THE TURNING POINT

Almost every great band story has a turning point. It could be a chance meeting with someone influential or a concert where everything just clicked and the band took off. It is that point where the years of rehearsing suddenly start to pay off.

For Elton John, it was a gig at the famous Troubadour on Santa Monica Boulevard in West Hollywood. He had already recorded two albums in the United Kingdom, and "Your Song" was climbing the charts in America. But on August 25, 1970, he played in the United States for the first time, hosting the first of a six-night series at the Troubadour. The reviews were amazing, and suddenly Elton John went from a nearly unknown to a must-see act.

Fleetwood Mac had already had some substantial success as a blues band when their turning point arrived. Although they were popular in blues circles, they were pretty much invisible to the mainstream in 1975. That's when Mick Fleetwood met Lindsey Buckingham, and invited him and his then-girlfriend Stevie Nicks to join the band. The following year they recorded *Rumours*, one of the bestselling albums in history.

KISS went from obscurity to the pinnacle of rock 'n' roll,

and the turning point was on March 9, 1973, when they unveiled their comic book characters, donned makeup, and created a theatrical stage show unlike anything else. At that moment, they turned a corner and immediately started to get noticed. It took only two years to become a top-flight rock act.

Trader Joe's, a chain of neighborhood grocery stores that consistently ranks among the highest in customer service, came to a turning point in 1967 when founder Joe Coulombe was on vacation in the Caribbean. He had been running a chain of stores called Pronto Market in Los Angeles for eleven years. In 1967 he created the character of "Trader Joe" to make his stores stand out from other local convenience stores. Today there are 353 Trader Joe's locations across the country.

The turning point for McDonald's, the largest fast-food restaurant chain, came when Ray Kroc opened sixty-eight new stores in 1959 and then launched a major advertising blitz that encouraged drivers to "look for the Golden Arches." That expansion more than doubled the number of McDonald's restaurants in the nation. The subsequent advertising campaign set the tone for the company's aggressive marketing strategy that exists to this day worldwide.

At some point, every rock star brand finds that moment of transition when the kindling catches fire and the tiny flame becomes a massive blaze. Great brands recognize opportunity and seize the day, like Ray Kroc and Joe Coulombe did.

MAKING IT ON THE WORLD STAGE

It's been suggested that getting to the top is easy, but staying there is the real challenge. Once a brand has reached a certain level of success, how do you keep it moving forward?

The story of AC/DC shows just how important consistency is. AC/DC recognized what their fans expected of them and then faithfully delivered on it in every concert, every album, and every song. They will probably retire before they risk letting down their fans.

Staying at the top is a tricky balance of living up to customer expectations at all times, while simultaneously evolving and growing in order to avoid stagnation. The urge to undergo major change can be a deliciously tempting one, but for rock star brands it should happen gently.

Even in the electronics industry, where change happens lightning fast and standing still can kill a company, rock star brands manage growth and change carefully. Each generation of Apple's iPhone or iPad is built on the premise that the original can be improved upon, not radically redesigned.

Coke, no question a rock star brand itself, made one of the legendary branding blunders when they altered their traditional formula and unveiled "New Coke" in 1985. Despite marketing research that indicated more than 80 percent of tasters preferred the new taste of Coke, backlash was swift and severe. Less than three months after launching New Coke amid tremendous fanfare, Coke brought back their traditional formula. Coke executives were open about the fact that they grossly underestimated the emotional attachment that consumers had to the historic brand.

Every rock star brand needs to remember to approach change cautiously, and always consider it from the customer's point of view. Once a consumer's heart is made up, it's nearly impossible to change. Remember the New Coke debacle and never forget that when it comes to consumers' purchasing decisions, the heart always trumps the mind.

▼

ACKNOWLEDGMENTS

Writing a book is not a solo album. I am extremely grateful to those who made these pages possible and to those who made it better along the way. There's no way I could possibly thank everyone personally in this small space.

Thanks to my parents for giving me, either by design or pure luck, the urge to tell stories and the courage to believe that if I did, someone would listen.

Thank you to Rob Steele, Dave Murray, and the exceptional team at Newcap Radio for believing in this crazy project from the beginning.

Thanks to the readers and contributors to the *Brand Like a Rock Star* blog for helping this book take shape. I am extremely grateful for the many selflessly brilliant minds I have been fortunate to come into contact with.

Finally, thank you to the music and radio industries, which have blessed me with the chance to make a living doing something I love. Because of you, I haven't had to go to "work" in nearly thirty years. Let's keep it that way.

ABOUT THE AUTHOR

Steve has spent nearly thirty years creating powerful radio brands in the US, Canada, and the Caribbean. He has had a front row seat to the rise—and sometimes the fall—of some of rock 'n' roll's biggest stars. Those insights form the foundation of his debut book *Brand Like a Rock Star*. Bringing together his mutual love of music and marketing, Steve takes you onstage, backstage, and behind the scenes with rock's biggest stars to reveal how their experiences can help your business become more profitable and more famous. Using the stories behind stars like AC/DC, U2, Bob Dylan, Lady Gaga, Jimmy Buffett, KISS, and the Grateful Dead, Steve shows you how to build a brand that rocks.

As a speaker and consultant, Steve has helped businesses of all sizes develop stronger bonds with their customers by creating solid brands. His blog at www.brandlikearockstar.com has thousands of readers in countries around the globe. When he isn't speaking, writing, and rockin', Steve is vice president of programming for Newcap Radio, overseeing content on over eighty radio stations. Steve is an avid hockey player, traveler, scuba diver, and pilot. He lives on Canada's east coast, just outside Halifax, Nova Scotia, with his wife Susan and their two boys, Isaac and Matthew. If you press shuffle on his iPod, you are most likely to hear Bob Marley.

Steve would love to speak to your company or conference about branding, marketing, and how to use rock 'n' roll to build your business.

Please contact him at steve@brandlikearockstar.com or visit www.brandlikearockstar.com.